## 1908

*Santa Claus, 1909*

Often, as the short winter day drew to a close, the family gathered round the fire (for the house was none too warm) and the children would listen intently to father as he told stories of Denmark's heroes, or tales of Vikings bold. These and Norse sagas were repeated again and again, until the childish listeners knew them almost by heart, but oft telling never seemed to rob them of their charm. Frequently, the twilight hour was given over to music, and father, who had a fine voice, sang the hymns and songs that he and mother had learned to love. Often, he would bring out his mouth-organ and play lively, rollicking tunes, keeping time gaily with his foot as he played. The recital over, mother lit the lamp and placed supper on the table. — *Kate Johnson*    H. Robertson, *Salt of the Earth,* pp. 66-67

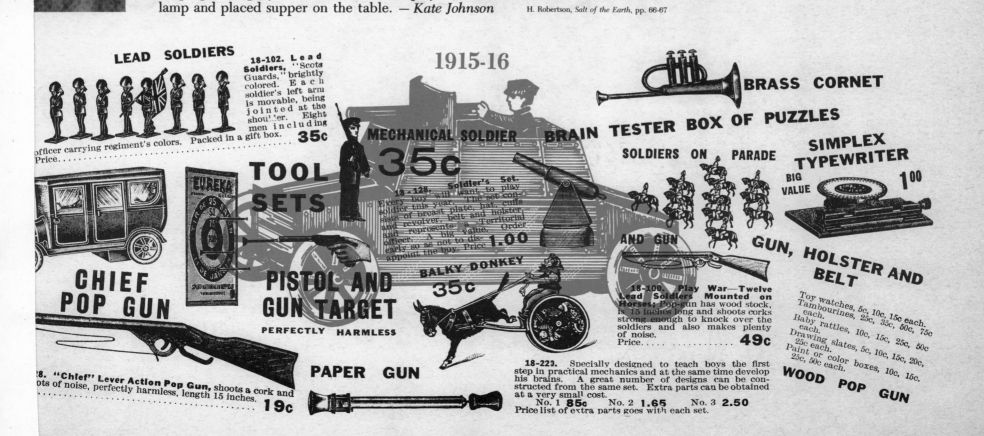

## 1915-16

# SCHOOL DAYS

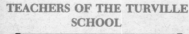

Miss R. R. Talbot was the first teacher, her salary was $45.00 per month.

*Wagon Trails to Hard Top, p. 345*

*Children working in a school garden plot near Airdrie, Alberta.*

Children came from miles away on foot and on horseback. There were no "Light Horse Clubs" in those days, but nearly every child was a horseback rider by the time he was of school age. Since most of the horses that had been brought into the country with the settlers had died of swamp fever, oxen and Indian Cayuses were used to take their place. Cayuses were hardy and tough and could rustle for themselves but many of them never were really broken, were difficult to catch and ready to buck every time they were ridden. To stay on one of them, and to get to school following trails blazed through standing timber; to navigate treacherous sloughs and mud—holes and broken corduroy; to open and close countless gates, of individual and complicated design, and in all stages of repair; and to arrive at school safely and on time, was no small part of a child's education in the easy years. In winter, lunches would be frozen. So also, was the water in the bucket, and the ink, and often cheeks, ears, fingers, or noses. Lessons would be heard around the big black wood heater until the room began to warm up.

*Wagon Trails to Hard Top, p. 806*

*Ottawa, 1906*

## TEACHERS OF THE TURVILLE SCHOOL

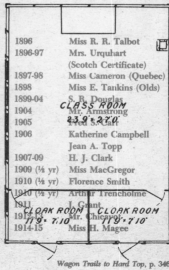

| | |
|---|---|
| 1896 | Miss R. R. Talbot |
| 1896-97 | Mrs. Urquhart (Scotch Certificate) |
| 1897-98 | Miss Cameron (Quebec) |
| 1898 | Miss E. Tankins (Olds) |
| 1899-04 | S. R. Douglas |
| 1904 | Mr. Armstrong |
| 1905 | M. S. Carr |
| 1906 | Katherine Campbell |
| | Jean A. Topp |
| 1907-09 | H. J. Clark |
| 1909 (½ yr) | Miss MacGregor |
| 1910 (½ yr) | Florence Smith |
| 1910 (½ yr) | Arthur Trencholme |
| 1911 | J. Grant |
| 1913 | Mr. Chisorn |
| 1914-15 | Miss H. Magee |

*Wagon Trails to Hard Top, p. 346*

## First Lesson in English
*(Adapted from Kyriak's novel, Sons of the Soil)*

Goodwin walked into the schoolroom and found all the people lined up against the walls, hats off as if before a king or bishop. On some faces there was an inexplicable look of hostility. Some of the shyer boys and girls had fled into the woods. But all the parents had come, determined to see for themselves whether the teacher were not going to "eat his bread for nothing."

"Sit down," said Goodwin to the children, giving them a sign with his hand that they should be seated.

The children looked at one another and at Goodwin and did not sit.

"Sit down," commanded Goodwin again, and himself took a seat. Some of the children sat down; others did not know what to do.

"Sit down, why are you standing?" cried out Cornelius Vorkun in Ukrainian. The children all sat down.

"Stand up!" said Goodwin, standing.

The children looked uncertainly at Cornelius and, seeing that he stood, they also arose.

"Sit down!" cried the teacher.

And now Cornelius saved the situation. He sat down, and so did the whole class.

"Stand up! Sit down! Stand up! Sit down!" Goodwin commanded several times, and the children, caught up in the rhythm of the thing, stood up and sat down with great relish—they had taken a fancy to this kind of "learning."

"Stand up!" called Goodwin, The children stood.

V. Lysenko, *Men in Sheepskin Coats*, p. 61

*Ottawa, 1909*

*Edmonton Public School, c. 1906*

*Sikh immigrants from India were refused entry at Vancouver and held aboard ship for two weeks*

The French Canadian community was never in favour of a large influx of immigrants. They were first of all interested in maintaining the autonomy of Quebec, in the preservation of their national culture and of the natural resources of their province.   S. I. Belkin, *Through Narrow Gates*, p. 8

The non-Anglo-Saxon has shouldered the burden as the Canadian man-of-all-work. He is doing seven-tenths of all the coal-mining and seventy-eight per cent of all the work in the woollen mills. Eighty-five per cent of all labour in slaughter-house and meat-packing industries is non-British. He makes about nineteen-twentieths of all clothing and four-fifths of all furniture. He turns out eighty per cent of all the leather and one-half of the gloves, and refines almost all the sugar. Wherever he is, he is the backbone of industry. He engages in all the dangerous occupations and he takes on the hard, unpleasant jobs which the Canadian workman is glad to relinquish; in every Province of Canada he is forcing his way to the forefront in agriculture, Canada's chief industry.
V. Lysenko, *Men in Sheepskin Coats*, p. 89

In 1903 demands were voiced in the Eastern Provinces that Western Canada should be held for native born rather than for Europeans or American settlers. In the same year a group of Montreal French Canadian citizens, under the leadership of Olivar Asselin, formed the Canadian National League which, amongst other things, began agitating in an organized manner against the foreign born.   S. I. Belkin, *Through Narrow Gates*, p. 7

Canada has been the dumping ground for thousands of undesirable immigrants—from the slums of the British cities, from Austria, Poland and other European countries. She is also the victim of colonies of sects who refuse to become assimilated—to become Canadian. This must stop. Our asylums and jails are over full of degenerates, criminals, and mental defectives...   R. Harvey and H. Troper, *Immigrants*, p. 740

# SOME ANXIOUS CANADIANS

In the coast cities of Vancouver and Victoria and New Westminster there are at least seven factories carrying on an extensive business in opium manufacturing. It is estimated that the annual gross receipts of these combined concerns amount for the year 1907, to between $600,000 and $650,000. The crude opium is imported from India in coconut shells, it is "manufactured" by a process of boiling into what is termed "powdered" opium and subsequently into opium "prepared for smoking". The returns show that large amounts of crude opium have been imported annually, and that large amounts of crude opium imported in the nine months of the fiscal year of 1906-1907 was greater than the value of the amount in the twelve months of the preceding year; the figures for these periods being $262,818 and $261,943, respectively.

The factories are owned and the entire work of manufacture is carried on by Chinese, between 70 and 100 persons being employed. One or two of the factories have been in existence for over twenty years, but the majority have been recently established. It is asserted by the owners of these establishments that all the opium manufactured is consumed in Canada, by Chinese and white people, but there are strong reasons for believing that much of what is produced at the present time is smuggled into China, and the coast cities of the United States. However, the amount consumed in Canada, if known, would probably appall the ordinary citizen who is inclined to believe that the habit is confined to the Chinese, and by them indulged in only to a limited extent.

The Chinese with whom I associated and conversed on the subject, assured me that almost as much opium was sold to white people as to Chinese and that the habit of opium smoking was making headway, not only among white men and boys, but also among women and girls. I saw evidences of the truth of these statements in my round of visits through some opium dens of Vancouver.   Canada, Parliament. House of Commons. *Sessional Papers*, p. 7

*Vancouver, 1907*

*Processional Arch built in honour of the Duke of Connaught, c. 1908.*

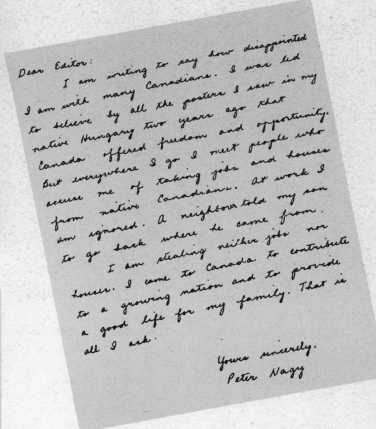

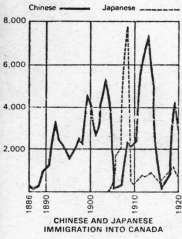

CHINESE AND JAPANESE
IMMIGRATION INTO CANADA

C. J. Woodsworth, *Canada and the Orient*, p. 119

## THE DOCKERS AT PT. EDWARD OBJECT TO THE FOREIGNERS

### One Hundred Longshoremen Employed by Northern Navigation Company Quit Work When Staff Is Augmented by a Number of Bulgarians and Italians.

[Special to The Advertiser.]

Sarnia, April 28. Because they say they object to working alongside foreigners, 100 longshoremen employed at the Point Edward docks by the Northern Navigation Company went on strike last night. The men are employed day and night at the rate of 25 cents an hour. Recently the company decided that it required a larger staff, and consequently 28 foreigners, principally Bulgarians and Italians, arrived on the scene last night, and were at once put to work. The regular staff immediately quit, declaring they would not return to work until the new men are dropped. The real reason appears to be that they fear the company may cut the rate of wages if they can secure a sufficient number of non-union dockers.

*London Advertiser*, 28 Apr. 1910, p. 8

Jews from Hungary and Italians from Palermo moved into the tiny cottage houses of Chestnut St. where, on summer weekend afternoons, they affably greeted one another in mutually unintelligible tongues. Now and again, they shyly exchanged gifts—a bottle of dark red wine for a steaming hot loaf of chala.

Russian Jews and more Italians lived side by side on Centre Ave. where proximity to the Harrison public baths was a major selling point in a neighborhood in which three-quarters of the houses lacked indoor plumbing.     R. Corelli, *The Toronto That Used To Be*, pp. 47-48

Then there is the green Emigrant that comes out of the European Cities that know nothing about farming, and they will squat on the ranchers land and annoy them, while if we could be left alone for a while as the farmers are we would make this business a credit to ourselves, and the Government would be proud of the showing we make. We are almost all Canadians, while the people that are squatting are almost all Foreigners.     L. G. Thomas, *The Prairie West*, p. 281

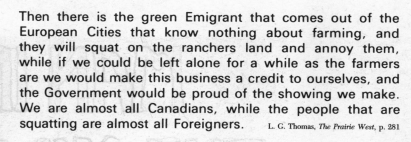

The first parties of Ukrainian immigrants to the mines were sometimes used as strike-breakers or as "reserves" to be thrown in, in case of a strike. This was also true of the Italians who were brought into the mines for that purpose. In this rôle they earned the ill will of other workers, although later they became active in union organization. They were sent to the remotest territories, and given all the hardest work, since the former peasant had no industrial skills. Often they were paid only half what the other workers were paid, especially the so-called "Old Canadians." This created hatred and grudges. On the accusation that they brought down wages, other workers fell upon them, beat them up, and drove them from work. Often they had to undertake a contract that they would not leave until they had worked off transportation and paid off the agent; when they tried to escape, they had to walk hungry through the forests for hundreds of miles, begging for food, or driving off attacks of dogs set upon them.

V. Lysenko, *Men in Sheepskin Coats*. pp. 93-94

Q. Are there any Italians doing tailoring work?
A. They take the work home, and they run what are known as sweating shops. They are making quite a pile of money...
Q. Do they do the work cheaper than regular men?
A. They do the work cheaper, and they get women to do the work cheaper still.

*Royal Commission on the Relations Between Capital and Labour*, Vol. V, p. 628

# In 1910 Canada is Asked by Great Britain to Provide Financial Help to Build up Her Navy

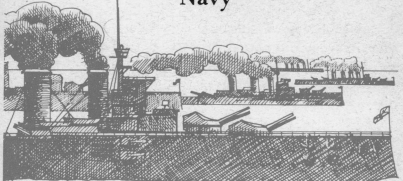

## A FRENCH VIEW

It is becoming apparent that despite all his declarations to the contrary, the Prime Minister is determined to drive us into the arms of the British even further. Not content with the folly of involving Canadians in the South African War he now seems bent upon committing Canadian money and blood to every British conflict and petty squabble from the seas in China to the coasts of the Baltic.

## AN ENGLISH VIEW

Dear Sir:

It should never be forgotten that our mother country Britain should always be able to rely on Canadians for assistance in times of trouble. Laurier's response to Britain's request for Naval aid is an insult to all the principles of the British Empire. Outright donations of money to Britain would have been far more useful than Laurier's "tin pot navy".

Sincerely,

A Concerned Canadian

## LAURIER AND THE NAVAL BILL

The bill ... provides for the creation of a naval force to be composed of a permanent corps, a reserve force, and a volunteer force ...

The Act provides that ... in the case of war ... the force may be called into active service. There is also an important provision ... that while the naval force is to be under the control of the Canadian government ... yet, in case of emergency the Governor in Council may place at the disposal of His Majesty for general service in the royal navy ...    House of Commons, *Debates*, 12 January 1910, cols. 1733-1734.

|  | 1908 | | | 1911 | | |
|---|---|---|---|---|---|---|
|  | C | L | Other | C | L | Other |
| Alberta | 3 | 4 | – – | 1 | 6 | – – |
| British Columbia | 5 | 2 | – – | 7 | – – | – – |
| Manitoba | 8 | 2 | – – | 7 | 2 | 1 |
| New Brunswick | 2 | 11 | – – | 5 | 8 | – – |
| Northwest Terr. | | | | | | |
| Nova Scotia | 6 | 12 | – – | 9 | 9 | – – |
| Ontario | 48 | 36 | 2 | 72 | 13 | 1 |
| Prince Edward Is. | 1 | 3 | – – | 2 | 2 | – – |
| Quebec | 11 | 53 | 1 | 27 | 37 | 1 |
| Saskatchewan | 1 | 9 | – – | 1 | 9 | – – |
| Yukon | – – | 1 | – – | 1 | – – | – – |
|  | 85 | 133 | 3 | 132 | 86 | 3 |

# In 1911 the Main Election Issue was Reciprocity with the United States

**THE EFFECT OF THE "NATIONAL POLICY."**

**(A PICTURE FROM REAL LIFE.)**

The original of this picture, called "Mortgaging the Homestead," is a painting by the celebrated Canadian artist, G. A. Reid, and is now in the Art Gallery at Ottawa.

The figures to the right represent the old couple, who as pioneers cleared the farm from the bush, while the son, who has failed to make "both ends meet," is signing the Mortgage Deed of the "Old Homestead" The picture of the old folks is one of hopeless resignation, while that of the young wife is expressive of fierce anger at the sad ending of her husband's labours.

**FARMERS AND FARMERS' WIVES, LOOK AT THIS PICTURE!**
Men, Vote for your own welfare—Reform, Unrestricted Reciprocity and Farmers Rights.

## BORDEN'S PLATFORM

And let us never forget that Canada cannot become commercially a part of the United States and remain politically a part – and an important part – of the British Empire.

We must decide whether the spirit of Canadianism or Continentalism shall prevail on the Northern half of this continent.

With Canada's youthful vitality, her rapidly increasing population, her marvellous material resources, her spirit of hopefulness and energy, she can place herself within a brief period in the highest position within the mighty Empire. This question is above all parties and all individuals. I appeal to Liberals as the Conservatives, and I speak to them not as a party leader, but as a Canadian citizen whose hopes are bound up with the hopes of his country.    R. C. Brown and M. E. Prang, *Confederation to 1949.*

## LAURIER'S PLATFORM

I stated a moment ago that the agreement we made, is simply to get better prices for the product of the Canadian farmers. This is a proposition so obvious that I am surprised it should have received the treatment it has received on the part of our friends opposite. But the objections to this agreement are not to be found ... they are all based on (irrelevant) grounds. I think I am fair in stating that the objections made to this arrangement are fourfold. The first objection is that the effect will be to deflect the carrying trade from Canadian channels to American channels. The second is that it will destroy our natural resources. The third is that it will imperil our industries. And the fourth is that it will land us ultimately in the American Republic.

(Laurier then went on to present a lengthy, detailed argument against these four objections).

Wilfrid Laurier, House of Commons *Debates*, 1910-1911, March 7, pp. 4754-4771.

# ACKNOWLEDGEMENTS

The authors would like to take this opportunity to acknowledge a number of people for their valuable assistance in the preparation of the manuscript. Our thanks to Dr. Douglas Laur, Faculty of Education, University of Western Ontario, who helped us develop an understanding of education for the period; to Ms Vera Senchuk of the Public Archives for patience assistance; to Dr. Carl Christie of British Records and Manuscript Section who helped us cope with the labyrinth of the archives and whose extra work prevented several repeated trips to Ottawa. A special thanks goes to our wives, Laura and Maureen.

Rob Greenaway, Associate Editor, Julian Cleva, Art Director and Wilda Lossing and Joan McCracken, Production Editors, all of Prentice-Hall, deserve special thanks for their suggestions and assistance. Sources of original material include the City of Toronto Archives, the Glenbow-Alberta Institute, the Government of Ontario Archives, London Public Library, the Public Archives of Canada, the Saskatchewan Archives, the United Church Archives and the University of Western Ontario.

# BIBLIOGRAPHY AND CREDITS

## PHOTOGRAPHS

The abbreviations for arrangement on each page are: T = 7
M = Middle, B = Bottom, combined when necessary with
R = Right, and L = Left.
p. 2 TL: Glenbow-Alberta Institute NA-2407-7; ML: GAI
1430-2; B: Public Archives of Canada C63087; MR: PAC
C63482; p. 3 ML: GAI NA-1421-6; T: PAC C63084; B: P/
C63469; p. 4 Top to Bottom: C89542, C89538, C89534,
C89537; p. 5 Clockwise from TL: C89531, C89536, C8953
C89541, C89533, C89532, C89540, C89539; p. 6 T: PAC
C68842; B: PAC PA10226; p. 7 T: PAC C5628; B: PAC
PA21324; p. 8 T: PAC PA10237; B: PAC PA20911; p. 9 M
PAC PA41785; T: PAC C4745; B: PAC PA10398; p. 10 T
GAI NA-1255-30; B: GAI NA-1687-38; pp. 10-11 T: GAI N
1255-20; p. 11 ML: Saskatchewan Archives B3275(2); MR:
C38424; B: GAI NA-2412-13; pp. 12-13 PAC PA50909; p.
PAC C11390; M: GAI NA-1334-2; pp. 14-15 B: PAC PA38
p. 15 MR: PAC PA37813; p. 16 M: PAC C37323; p. 17 T:
C8702; M: GAI NA-586-2; B: GAI NA-1199-1; p. 18 T: P/
PA73691; M: GAI NA-2284-15; B: PAC C68840; p. 19 T:
C681; M: GAI NA-1130-9; B: GAI NA-1438-4; p. 20 T: P/
C44126; M: PAC C25884; BL: PAC PA29387; pp. 20-21 B
Ontario Archives S5198; p. 21 T: OA L1407; M: PAC
PA98657; BR: OA S8660; p. 22 T: OA L1427; MR: PAC
PA73567; BL: GAI NA-1504-9; BR: OA L1423; B: OA L1·
p. 23 TR: PAC C14968; TL: OA L1423; ML: OA L1423;
OA L1427; BL: PAC PA18584; BR: OA L1427; p. 24 T: P
C80430; B. City of Toronto Archives Health #3; p. 25 M
PAC C30936; B. PAC PA30820; p. 26 T: PAC C30945; M
PAC PA29182; B: CTA Sewers #42; pp. 26-27 B: PAC
C38715; p. 27 T: PAC PA74737; M: PAC PA98848; p. 28
GAI NA-1608-11; B: PAC C43519; pp. 28-29 M: PAC C4
p. 29 T: PAC PA38495; B: GAI NA-2816-4; p. 30 M: G/
334-6; p. 31 T: PAC PA44506; B: OA; p. 32 M: PAC C
pp. 32-33 M: PAC C18999; p. 33 T: PAC PA12059; p. 3
OA S15592; p. 37 T: OA S13447; p. 38 T: PAC PA2793
OA P2158; B: PAC PA28621; p. 39 T: PAC PA29178; M
P2156; BL: OA P2257; BR: OA P2214; p. 40 PAC C309
41 PAC RD55; p. 42 TL: GAI NA-3154-3; BL: PAC PA
BR: GAI NA-2858-8; pp. 42-43 M: PAC PA23095; B: P/
PA11515; p. 43 TR: PAC C68792; BR: PAC PA28236;
PAC PA34014; pp. 44-45 B: PAC C23555; p. 45 T: PA
C17812; B: PAC C8805; p. 46 PA 25998; p. 47 OA P20

*Every reasonable effort has been made to find copyright*
*of quotations. The publishers would be pleased to have a*
*errors or omissions brought to their attention.*

## GOVERNMENT PUBLICATIONS

*Board of Inquiry into the Cost of Living. Report to the Board*
*1915.* Ottawa: Department of Labour, Statistical Branch,
Government of Canada.
Canada. Parliament. House of Commons. *Sessional Papers.* 42,
Vol. 17, No. 36b, Ottawa: King's Printer, 1908.
*Canada West.* Ottawa: Minister of the Interior, Government of
Canada, 1913.
*Canada West: The Last Best West.* Ottawa: Minister of
Agriculture, Government of Canada, 1908.
*Canada Year Book 1906.* Ottawa: Census and Statistics Office,
Government of Canada.
*Canada Year Book 1913.* Ottawa: Census and Statistics Office,
Government of Canada.
*Canada Year Book 1914.* Ottawa: Census and Statistics Office,
Government of Canada.
*Census of Canada 1931.* Ottawa: Dominion Bureau of
Statistics, Government of Canada.
*Department of Labour, Wages, and Hours of Labour in*
*Canada, 1901* Ottawa: Department of Labour,
Government of Canada.
*Department of Labour, Wages, and Hours of Labour in*
*Canada, 1920.* Ottawa: Department of Labour,
Government of Canada.
*Labour Gazette.* Ottawa: Department of Labour, Government
of Canada, 1905.

## PERIODICALS

*e Canadian Churchman*
*nadian Magazine*
*balt Daily Nugget*
*monton Bulletin*
*monton Journal*
*ndon Advertiser*
*ntreal Star*
*ronto Star*
*ronto Evening Telegram*
*estern Home Monthly*
*nnipeg (Manitoba) Free Press*

*Women's Work in Western Canada.* The Canadian Pacific
Railway Company, 1906.
Young, Charles Hurlburt and Helen R. Y. Reid. *The Japanese*
*Canadians.* Toronto: University of Toronto Press, 1938.

# A NATION BECKONS : CANADA 1896-1914

**DOUGLAS H. FAIRBAIRN**
*South Secondary School, London*

**GRAHAM L. BROWN**
*Montcalm Secondary School, London*

PRENTICE-HALL OF CANADA, LTD., SCARBOROUGH, ONTARIO

## CONTENTS

**160 ACRE FARMS IN WESTERN CANADA FREE**

## Health, Liberty and Prosperity
### Await the Settler in the Prairie Provinces of Alberta, Saskatchewan and Manitoba
*Canadian Magazine, Jan. 1907, p. 29*

**WESTER** Produces the M GRAIN, ROO

There has been . . . extraordinary demand in recent years for farm help in the Province of Ontario, and in order to assist as far as possible in meeting this demand the plan will be tried this year of employing agents on commission. We have in view somewhere in the neighborhood of 200 men residing in agricultural centres in this province, who will, I think, be found willing and able to render valuable assistance in the distribution of immigrants of the farm laborer classes.

J. S. Woodsworth, *Strangers Within Our Gates*, p. 177

The excellent crop of 1905, it is claimed, will put fully $60,000,000 in circulation in Western Canada, and it is freely stated that the great expenditure in railway construction at present going on will raise that amount to $100,000,000 during the current year—which will bring added prosperity to the country that lies between Winnipeg and the foothills.

*Canadian Magazine, June 1909, p. 30*

The following is a statement showing immigration literature ordered by the Immigration Department during the nine months ending 31 March, 1906:

| | |
|---|---:|
| Gaelic pamphlet | 10,000 |
| The Canadian West | 1,500 |
| Symposium of Ideas and Prophecies | 1,500 |
| The Canadian West | 100,000 |
| Reliable Information | 2,000 |
| Western Canada, a Land of Unequalled Opportunities | 2,000 |
| Great Growth of Western Canada | 2,000 |
| Western Canada, a Land of Unprecedented Progress | 2,000 |
| Book of Lectures | 200 |
| The Story of Western Canada Crop | 300,000 |
| Farm and Ranch Review | 5,000 |
| Canadian Year Book | 5,000 |
| Prince Edward Island pamphlet | 30,000 |
| Immigration Act | 40,000 |
| Canada in a Nutshell | 100,000 |
| Home Building in Canada | 115,000 |
| Classes Wanted in Canada | 50,000 |
| Land Regulations | 50,000 |
| Canada Wants Domestic Servants | 50,000 |
| A Travers le Canada | 20,000 |
| Illustrated Pamphlet of Winnipeg | 1,000 |
| Everyman's Geology of Three Prairie Provinces of the Canadian West | 5,000 |
| Eastern Townships | 30,000 |
| Reduced Rates for Settlers | 100,000 |
| How to Succeed in Canada | 200,000 |
| Canada, Work, Wages and Land (English) | 200,000 |
| Canada, Work, Wages and Land (Danish) | 20,000 |
| Canada, Work, Wages and Land (Norwegian) | 20,000 |
| Canada, Work, Wages and Land (Finnish) | 20,000 |
| Canada, Work, Wages and Land (German) | 20,000 |
| Canada, Work, Wages and Land (Swedish) | 20,000 |
| Canada, Work, Wages and Land (French) | 20,000 |
| Canada, Work, Wages and Land (Belgian) | 20,000 |
| Canada, the Land of Opportunity (English) | 200,000 |
| Canada, the Land of Opportunity (Swedish) | 50,000 |
| Canada, the Land of Opportunity (Norwegian) | 50,000 |
| Canada, the Land of Opportunity (Finnish) | 50,000 |
| Canada, the Land of Opportunity (Danish) | 50,000 |
| Canada, the Land of Opportunity (Flemish) | 50,000 |
| Canada, the Land of Opportunity (French) | 50,000 |
| Western Canada | 500 |
| Climate of Canada | 500 |
| Western Canada Early Days | 500 |
| Western Canada Crop Prospects | 500 |
| What Canada Possesses | 500 |
| Letters from Successful Settlers (French) | 20,000 |
| Hangers | 50,000 |
| Facts for Settlers | 100,000 |
| Last Best West | 375,000 |

*J. S. Woodsworth, Strangers Within Our Gates, p. 115*

From the annual report I learn that the Ottawa Valley Immigration Aid Society arranged for ten lectures, and directed the placing of 661 settlers—350 in New Ontario, 190 in New Quebec, and 121 in the Western Provinces.

*J. S. Woodsworth, Strangers Within Our Gates, p. 177*

'Whatever is bringing you to Canada?' I queried, and a dozen fellows crowded around our seats. 'The same thing that is bringing all the boys,' was the answer. 'We want work,' and he roared out laughing, as if it was a great joke. 'That's right, isn't it?' and the boys all echoed, 'It was work.'

J. S. Woodsworth, *Strangers Within Our Gates*, p. 59

I applied for one job. When I got there one hundred and fifty were standing in line. I sidled up to the porter. "Get in line," he tells me. "I say, governor," I asks him, "how many have been in already?" "About twice as many." I decided to look for another job, and that gay infectious laugh of his again echoed through the car. 'What's the chance of a job?' he asked.

J. S. Woodsworth, *Strangers Within Our Gates*, p. 59

'Why have I come to Canada? Well, that is easy. To get work. I haven't earned a penny since Christmas. I have walked twenty miles a day looking for a job. For every position that is open there are hundreds of applicants. They actually have to call out the police. I had been in one position twenty-eight years looking after the stud of a wealthy man. The governor died. The stables were sold. Every man of us was discharged; some there forty years, too. It was tough, I can tell you. I have been looking for work ever since.'

J. S. Woodsworth, *Strangers Within Our Gates*, p. 56

## Small criminal makes good ...

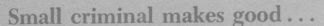

Eighteen months or so ago a lad was brought before the magistrates in ... Falmouth. He was charged with vagrancy, sleeping out, and having no visible means of subsistence. This was the third time he had been so charged, and he was only about sixteen years of age. The magistrates did not know what to do with him. They sent him to a poorhouse for a while. But when the time was up he was turned adrift again, and was very soon once more before the bench. But this time he was charged with attempting to commit suicide.... he went to Canada. And here is a letter which says of him: 'He is a fine fellow, doing well and greatly respected.' Now you have it in a nutshell; eighteen months ago he was starving and attempting suicide, and no one would give him work. Now he is greatly respected.

J. S. Woodsworth, *Strangers Within Our Gates*, pp. 54-55

The emigrants from Galicia are all proprietors of small holdings; the capital which they bring with them originates from the sales of their cottage garden and field. The field in Galicia is on an average worth about £13 per acre, the cottage with garden £20. The most candidates to emigration belong to the class of peasants holding three or four acres, because they can realize from sale of their property an amount sufficient to reach America, and because they find no difficulty in disposing of such small areas of land as about 4-5 acres among the remaining peasants of the village.

V. J. Kaye, *Early Ukrainian Settlements in Canada*, pp. 118-19

Did I ever farm? I should say not. I've lived in London all my life. I'm a railroad man. If I can't make farming go, perhaps I can get on the railroad. They say there are lots of railroad jobs.

J. S. Woodsworth, *Strangers Within Our Gates*, p. 57

To become the owner of 113 morgs of land may seem to many a bliss hoped for only in a dream. There is little doubt that it can be achieved, if only the emigration is properly organized. But there are many conditions which have to be fulfilled first, and which may prevent many of our people from achieving that happiness. First of all, there is the great distance to travel; transportation alone would cost 150 florins per person. The Canadian Government as a rule does not assist passages; immigrants have to defray the costs of transportation from their own funds. The crossing of the ocean lasts one week, and travel by rail in Europe and in Canada takes about 5 days. Inexperienced people are not advised to venture alone. It is best to travel in groups under the guidance of an experienced person who knows the language or who can at least speak German ... (2½ florins = $1.00)

V. J. Kaye, *Early Ukrainian Settlements in Canada*, p. 16

I have been out of work for three months. I was getting too hard up. I had to do something. Canada has been preached to us on every hand, so I decided to try my luck. I've walked hundreds of miles looking for work.

J. S. Woodsworth, *Strangers Within Our Gates*, p. 59

In order to make a living on the land given to them, one should have enough money to be able to live after arrival until the next crop is garnered, to be able to buy a pair of oxen for the ploughing, as well as implements for husbandry, or at least enough ready money to be able to hire a neighbour of longer standing to do the ploughing. The first settlers who emigrate must also have a few hundred florins in cash for the upkeep of their families. Those who arrive after them may be able to manage with less money, working on arrival for wages with farmers who came before them, and later, when they have acquired some knowledge of the language, they can be hired by other farmers. After a year they will earn so much cash that they will be able to take out their own homestead. (2½ florins = $1.00) V. J. Kaye, *Early Ukrainian Settlements In Canada*, p. 16

Night after night Pillipiw stayed up relating the fabulous tale.

"I told them of the wonders of the New World, laughing like mischief," related Pillipiw, as he rubbed his hands at the thought of the commission he was going to make, and the free machinery and household goods he would get free from the Canadian Government. V. Lysenko, *Men In Sheepskin Coats*, p. 18

...wheat — seas of it! And land! Did they know they could get 69½ hectares, 113 morgs, free! Who among the peasants ever had 113 morgs? V. Lysenko, *Men in Sheepskin Coats*, p. 17

"Flee, because here you have no land, and there is land! Here you are paupers; there, landowners." V. Lysenko, *Men in Sheepskin Coats*, p. 17

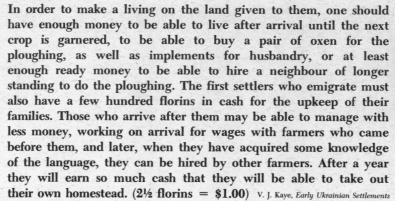

THE SMALL LANDOWNER
IN GALICIA
1882-1891

|  | florins |
|---|---|
| Value of Gross Grain Production | 112½ |
| **EXPENSES** | |
| Taxes, Rent, Feed (Yearly) | 50 |
| Value of Grain Set Aside for Spring Sowing | 30 |

SOME OTHER VARIABLE EXPENSES

Debt Payments
Insurance
Church Contributions
School Contributions
Building Repairs
Special Taxes to Build a New Church or School
Unforeseen Expenses
  – Accidents
  – Crop Failures
  – Deaths
  – Weddings

V. J. Kaye, *Early Ukrainian Settlements In Canada*, p.12

### LANDHOLDINGS IN GALICIA

| Year | No. of Large landowners | Avg. Holdings (hectares) |
|---|---|---|
| 1891 | 8448 | 3907 (967 acres) |
| 1902 | 235 | 7163 (17 731 acres) |

| 1859 | —the 788 234 landowners in Galicia averaged 5¼ hectares (13 acres) each. |
|---|---|
| 1898 | —30 000 small landowners 50% of whom held 2 hectares (5 acres) or less. |
| 1912 | —80% of all landowners held less than 1.6 hectares (4 acres). |
| 1912 | —1 200 000 people in Galicia whom the land would not support. |
|  | —2500 – 3000 farms per year were lost for debts of less than $40. |

V. J. Kaye, *Early Ukrainian Settlements In Canada*, p. 9

Steerage meals were apt to be entertaining — on one day ship pie was featured, with which one could carry on quite a game of 'what's this?'. It was evident it was composed of the left-overs from the upper crust's tables, hence one could get a taste of chicken and speculate if another bite was a piece of sausage.

H. Robertson, *Salt of the Earth*, p. 16

Every once in a while there'd be a fight and we'd all get around and egg them on. There'd be lots of singing. Some of the fellows played different instruments, fiddle and accordian and all in all we had a pretty nice time.

*P. S. Hordern, 1903, Barr Colony*

H. Robertson, *Salt of The Earth*, p. 14

The Saloon and Intermediate passengers are allowed to intermix, but Steerage are strictly kept to their own quarters. You soon get acquainted with everyone on board, as there is no formality. Most excellent grub was served and plenty of it. The bar was well patronized, champagne corks popped all day and far into the night, money was freely spent and a general air of festivity pervaded the whole ship.

*Charles Alfred Peyton, age 19, 1882, S. S. Circassian*

H. Robertson, *Salt of The Earth*, p. 17

# THE SEA VOYAGE

The ship was supposed to be a ship that would ordinarily carry 700 passengers and there were over 2,500 of us on board. There were a lot of goods being brought over. Everybody had a lot of things; some even brought their pianos.

H. Robertson, *Salt of The Earth*, p. 14

7 Days to go

4 Days to go

Quebec City

Halifax

The worst part of this trip was the lifeboat drill. The first time we did it there was near panic because everyone thought we were going to sink. I feared that after finally making the decision to go to Canada I would end up drowning in the Atlantic. I almost joined the women and children crying.

*A voyager.*

*Scottish immigrants, c. 1911*

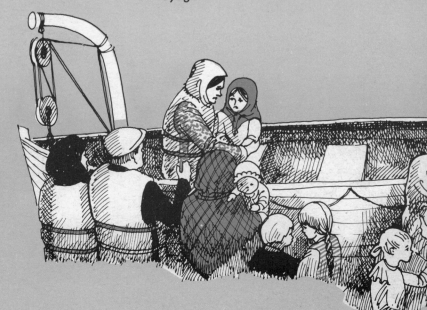

*Mealtime aboard the Lake Huron en route to Canada*

We were in what was called the forward hold. It was below the water line. As we walked down it looked pretty nice, all painted white inside, but when we got closer we saw that it was just whitewash. Later on when we got going the whitewash got knocked off the walls as the waves hit it. The whitewash would fall off in chunks and there was manure under it. It has been used to transport horses.

H. Robertson, *Salt of The Earth*, p. 14

FARES ON ALLAN LINE
LIVERPOOL TO CANADA
Saloon £10/10 to £18/18
Second Cabin £7/7
Steerage £4/10

Glasgow

Dublin

Liverpool

Southampton

Northern Europe

11 Days to go

4,360 Kilometres

4,561 Kilometres

8,784 Kilometres

We finally got on a boat that was a cattle boat fixed up with cabins from the stalls. Each cabin held four immigrants—two lower and two upper beds made of plain boards and straw mattresses and straw pillows.

H. Robertson, *Salt of The Earth*, p. 15

We got into the habit of hollering 'Duck!' when anyone got sick. The fellow underneath me was sitting reading one day when I got a spell and I leaned out to let go and the fellow across from me just happened to see it and hollered 'Duck!' and the fellow moved just in time. The guy below said, 'Why the devil don't you holler or whistle or something?' I said, 'How can I with my mouth full?'

H. Robertson, *Salt of The Earth*, p. 14

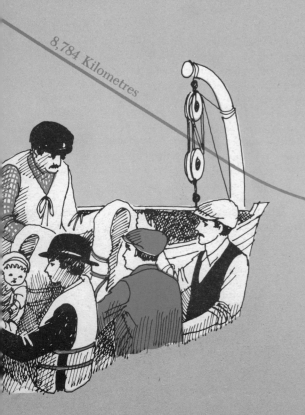

*Immigrants leaving Liverpool*

Adriatic

In August, 1891, the three travellers went through Lviv and Krakow to the border town, where a gendarme looked over their passports.

"Show me the money you have," he ordered. Pillipiw had 600 "rinski" ($240); Eleniak had 190 "rinski" ($76); and Panischak had only 120 ($48). Panischak was turned back, as he had insufficient money. He gave his money to the other two, who now travelled into Hamburg, where the German agent, Shapiro, sold them a passage to Winnipeg for $60 apiece. They had left some $244 to take them to the new country.

V. Lysenko, *Men In Sheepskin Coats*, p. 12

Waiting to go ashore at Quebec City, 1911

Here is a family of Poles; one child has 'weak eyes.' Of course she must be deported. But do we think what it means—the shock to the family when they learn that their little one is to be sent back and they are to go on. In spite of the father's and mother's grief the little girl is taken from them.
*J. S. Woodsworth, Strangers Within Our Gates, pp. 33-34*

# GATEWAY TO A NEW LIFE

## ARRIVALS IN CANADA
### SELECTED GROUPS, SELECTED YEARS

| NATIONALITIES | 1901 | 1905 | 1909 | 1913 |
|---|---|---|---|---|
| British | 11,810 | 65,359 | 52,901 | 150,542 |
| Austrian | 228 | 837 | 1,830 | 1,050 |
| French | 360 | 1,743 | 1,830 | 2,755 |
| Galician | 4,702 | 6,926 | 6,644 | 497 |
| Hebrew, Russian | – – | 6,206 | 1,444 | 6,304 |
| Italian | 4,710 | 3,473 | 4,228 | 16,601 |
| Japanese | 6 | 354 | 495 | 724 |
| Newfoundland | – – | 190 | 2,108 | 1,036 |
| Russian | 1,044 | 1,887 | 3,547 | 18,623 |
| Swedish | 485 | 1,847 | 1,135 | 2,477 |
| U.S. (Ocean Ports) | 68 | 109 | 94 | 121 |
| U.S. | 17,987 | 43,543 | 59,832 | 139,009 |

## DEPORTATIONS OF IMMIGRANTS AND PRINCIPAL CAUSES – SELECTED YEARS

| CAUSES | 1901 | 1905 | 1909 | 1913 |
|---|---|---|---|---|
| **Medical Causes:** | | | | |
| Insanity | | 2 | 13 | 22 |
| Mentally Retarded | | 3 | 27 | 21 |
| Tuberculosis | | 4 | 11 | 11 |
| Trachoma | | 486 | 94 | 72 |
| Hernia | | 1 | 3 | 13 |
| Other Medical Causes | | 28 | 41 | 107 |
| Accompanying Patients | | 13 | 60 | 28 |
| Contract Labour | NOT AVAILABLE | – – | – – | – – |
| Criminality | | 1 | 6 | 4 |
| Defective Sight | | – – | 17 | 9 |
| Immorality | | – – | 12 | 15 |
| Indirect Passage | | – – | – – | 45 |
| Lack of Funds | | – – | 67 | 204 |
| Likely to become a Public charge | | 56 | 292 | 56 |
| Poor Physique | | – – | 6 | 64 |
| Stowaway | | – – | 74 | 63 |
| Other Causes | | 13 | 5 | 17 |

*Canada Year Book, 1913*

*A boy awaiting deportation*

First comes the medical examination. Then all must pass through the 'cattle pen' – a series of iron-barred rooms and passage ways. They must go in single file, and each pass before various officials who question them as to their nationality and destination, and the amount of money they have in their possession. All this is very necessary, but it is a weary, anxious time. No one can tell what will come next. Many fear they will be stopped. Some are turned back – one taken and the others left. Now, there is the customs examination. At last tickets are arranged for, baggage transferred, and the immigrants find themselves bundled into a colonist car. This is another experience—not altogether a pleasant one either, since they are not accustomed to cooking and sleeping in such small quarters.
*J. S. Woodsworth, Strangers Within Our Gates, p. 34*

Only the other day one of the Government travelling agents had great difficulty in persuading a young fellow, before he started for the West, from investing some of his small capital in firearms and knives to kill the buffalo, wolves and other wild animals which his fellow passengers had persuaded him were to be encountered in the streets of Winnipeg. *J. S. Woodsworth, Strangers Within Our Gates, p. 36*

## MEDICAL OFFICERS
## LES OFFICIERS MEDICALS
## ÄRZTE
## DOKTOR
## LIJEČNIK

→

Fortunately, perhaps, the immigrant does not need to take the initiative, but finds himself carried along with the crowd. Management there must be, somewhere, and reason, doubtless, for all these tedious examinations, but he has no very clear idea as to the 'how' and 'why' of all that takes place during the long hours that elapse before he finds himself safely landed. His greatest anxiety is to look after his baggage. And what an assortment of boxes and bundles! No wonder that some pieces go astray!

J. S. Woodsworth, *Strangers Within Our Gates*, p. 34

Galician immigrants at the sheds, Quebec City

## A LETTER HOME

12 Rue de Roi
Montreal, Quebec
14 Aug. 1906

Dear Bridget

I arrived safely two weeks ago and got a job in sewer construction. I don't have enough money to go any further. I will save some money to send for you and the children. Then we can move to Saskatchewan. The work is dirty, but I am fine.

Your loving husband,
Mike Doherty

May 6, 1908

Sir:
There is at present in the Toronto Insane Asylum an Irish immigrant patient, named George Henry Gowdy, who arrived in Canada by Allan Line S.S. Sicilian on the 5th of February, 1906. This man is mentally deficient and likely to remain a permanent public charge unless sent home. His sister, who I understand has engaged passage by your line, will accompany him over.

Having come to Canada previous to 13th July, 1906, his case is not covered by the Immigration Act, but as it is desirable to get rid of him, the Department will pay charity rate for his transportation.

Will you kindly therefore make the necessary arrangement in steerage so that this man and his sister may travel together from Montreal.

Your obedient servant,
W. D. Scott
Superintendent of Immigration

Public Archives of Canada

Immigrants from Germany, 1911

*Settlers near Winnipeg*

...the second trainload of Emigrants leaving Cottonwood County Minnesota for Points in Western Canada, 67 cars have left mentioned County during the last two months and about that many more will follow before November 11th. *Canadian Magazine, Dec. 1905*

On approaching Winnipeg the other day a party of Scotch immigrants were having their homesick feelings stirred up by singing the old songs and somewhat sentimental speechifying; the women were in tears, and the men were feeling 'lumpy about the throat,' when a man at the other end of the car electrified the company and inspired new hope and cheerfulness by shouting out, 'what are ye dreeing aboot? Is't the poverty ye've left ahint? Think o' what's afore ye!'

J. S. Woodsworth, *Strangers Within Our Gates*, p. 37

## FREIGHT REGULATIONS

1)Carloads of settler's effects may be made up of the following described property: Live stock (not exceeding 10 head); household goods and personal property (second hand); wagons or other vehicles for personal use (second hand); farm machinery, implements and tools (all second hand); soft-wood lumber and shingles, which must not exceed 600 metres; or a Portable House may be shipped; seed grain, small quantity of trees or shrubbery; small lot live poultry or pet animals; and sufficient feed for the live stock while on journey. Settlers' Effects rates will not apply on shipments of second-hand wagons, buggies, farm machinery, implements or tools, unless accompanied by household goods.

2)Merchandise, such as groceries, provisions, hardware, etc., also implements, machinery, vehicles, etc., if new, will not be regarded as Settlers' Effects and will be charged regular rates.

*Canada West. The Last Best West*

HEADING WEST

One bright sunny morning, with the wind blowing a cold blast from the northwest, we loaded up a wagon, which included two pigs, a dozen hens, and as many necessities as possible, and started out, leading two cows, with a yearling colt running loose.

M. G. Moorhouse, *Buffalo Horn Valley*, p. 6

The immigrants were an odd lot. Or they seemed so, probably because they were bewildered by the language. They seemed to live on liverwurst. They carried everthing in wicker baskets. There was no point in trying to sell them anything worth more than five cents. It was the only coin they could recognize. Neekel? Neekel? Most kept their neekels in a pocket purse with a drawstring. On days when we had a couple of extra cars of immigrants, I was always assured of a good sale of apples. You couldn't ask much more than a neekel for an apple.

K. E. Liddell, *I'll Take the Train*, p. 13

*Emigrant family leaving railway station for homestead in Saskatchewan*

Horseplay was rough and the humor was crude, but the fellowship was genuine. In the earliest of years, farmers advised of arrivals, would line platforms of country stations to recruit help right from the coaches. The bargaining went on through the open windows.

K. E. Liddell, *I'll Take The Train*, p. 140

### Lost in the snow. . . .

W. C. Bruce, an old Hamilton man, but now of Tacoma, came out with his partner, Heber Smith, of Chicago. He reports that some 4,000 men spent the season on Copper river, and coming out in the middle of November over the Valdez glacier, quite a number of deaths occurred from the men being frozen to death. Among these were Harry Cohen, formerly a New York jeweler, who with nine companions started for the coast, and overcome by weakness, succumbed to the cold. His companion, named Smith, tried to get to the coast, but died from his injuries. Another young man, whose name could not be learned, froze to death, and a Hungarian, Geo. Poltovitch, who came on the Cottage City, lost part of each foot from frost bites. Smith and Khron were members of the same party. In company with several others they started across the glacier early in December. Smith was the first to freeze his feet. After they had crossed the summit and were going down the long stretch towards Valdez, his strength began to fail him . . .

George G. Sweezey, also of New York, was a blacksmith at Valdez for a long time. He started across the glacier early in the winter, drawing a heavy sled. The details of his death are unknown for he was alone.

The miners who arrived on the Cottage City say that many others perished like Sweezey. They are unable to give names. The men starting out in pairs or singly were never heard of again.

*Winnipeg Free Press,* 30 Jan. 1898, p. 2

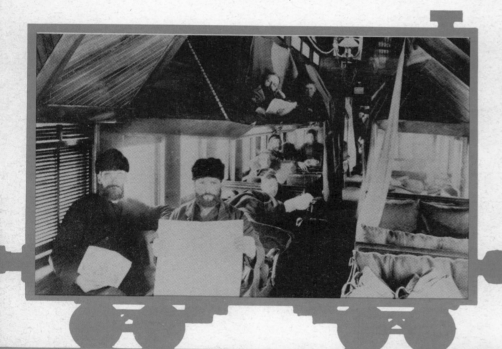
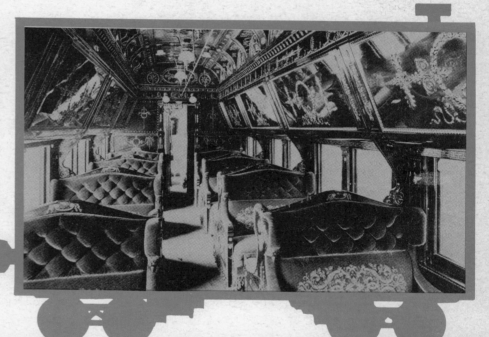

## An accident . . .

One day an immigrant train was brought to a sudden stop by an alarm from a Galician family that they had lost one of their children, a boy of eight, who had tumbled out of the window. All was interest and excitement, and the parents were loud in their expressions of dismay and grief, but as the train went slowly backward the young hopeful was discovered walking along the track and was finally picked up, quite unhurt, on perceiving which the parents experienced a sudden revulsion of feeling, and gave their offspring a vigorous whipping for the trouble he had caused by his escapade.       J. S. Woodworth, *Strangers Within Our Gates,* pp. 36-37

Every car has a stove set up at one end, together with a cistern of water, so that passengers can make tea and cook meals.

*Noel Copping, age 20, 1909,
Bulyea, Saskatchewan*

H. Robertson, *Salt of the Earth,* p. 20

There are a great many women and children on board and the prospects are there will be terrible suffering from hunger and cold. My enthusiasm for this glorious country is fast dying out and I would give anything for something to eat but there seems no hope of even getting a bite for the next 48 hours.

H. Robertson, *Salt of the Earth,* p. 18

*The possessions of J. J. Gulley of Ontario*

## 1902 SNOWFALL

|  | Amount (cm) | Days |
|---|---|---|
| January | 16 | 4 |
| February | 16.5 | 4 |
| March | 15 | 3 |
| April | .8 | 1 |
| May | 0 | 0 |
| June | 0 | 0 |
| July | 0 | 0 |
| August | 0 | 0 |
| September | 0 | 0 |
| October | 3.5 | 1 |
| November | 48 | 12 |
| December | 31 | 4 |

## THE WINTER OF 1902

|  | Mean Min. Monthly Temperature | Mean Max. Monthly Temperature | Low that Month |
|---|---|---|---|
|  | °C | °C | °C |
| November | −12 | −3 | −28 |
| December | −12 | −11 | −40 |
| January | −22 | −8 | −42 |
| February | −20 | −8 | −38 |

## THE SPRING OF 1902

|  | Mean Min. Monthly Temperature | Mean Max. Monthly Temperature | High that Month | Low that Month |
|---|---|---|---|---|
|  | °C | °C | °C | °C |
| March | −11 | 0 | 13 | −35 |
| April | −7 | 9 | 19 | −14 |
| May | 4 | 17 | 30 | −4 |

# YOUR NEW HOME

Scene and statistics near Lethbridge, Alberta

## THE SUMMER OF 1902

| | Mean Min. Monthly Temperature | Mean Max. Monthly Temperature | High that Month |
|---|---|---|---|
| | °C | °C | °C |
| June | 4 | 17 | 26 |
| July | 10 | 26 | 31 |
| August | 8 | 24 | 31 |

## THE FALL OF 1902

| | Mean Min. Monthly Temperature | Mean Max. Monthly Temperature | High that Month | Low that Month |
|---|---|---|---|---|
| | °C | °C | °C | °C |
| September | 0 | 16 | 26 | −11 |
| October | −2 | 10 | 22 | −13 |

## 1902 RAINFALL

| | Amount (cm) | Days |
|---|---|---|
| January | 0 | 0 |
| February | 0 | 0 |
| March | 2.2 | 3 |
| April | .15 | 1 |
| May | 7.4 | 9 |
| June | 19.5 | 26 |
| July | 7.8 | 13 |
| August | 2.5 | 3 |
| September | 2.8 | 12 |
| October | .7 | 2 |
| November | 1.7 | 1 |
| December | 0 | 0 |

## A Weekly Routine....

My way of life was very simple. I started off on Sunday by baking a gallon of pork and beans and enough bread to last a week. I would sweep the floor—if it needed it. Company never bothered me because I never had any. Weekdays I was up and had the bulls going by 4 o'clock in the morning, unhooked at nine and had lunch. Every second day I took two plowshares on my back and walked 12 miles to Baskervilles to have them sharpened—back home and had the bulls going at 4 p.m., unhooked at 9 p.m. had supper and went to bed. I did the same thing the next day and the next and the next. That summer in breaking 110 acres I walked some 880 miles.

H. Robertson, *Salt of the Earth*, p. 40

...plastered my sod house inside and out with clay dug from the well. I put flooring in it and as I had nothing else to do, I scrubbed it every other day and took out my bedding to air every morning. For music I stretched some brass wire on my home made bench and on this rude instrument I played little tunes. I even made verses to a tune I liked, a love song to my absent wife.

H. Robertson, *Salt of The Earth*, p. 29

*Ploughing with a dog team in the Northwest Territories*

# ESTABLISHING A HOME

### LAND REGULATIONS IN CANADA

1. A homestead may be taken up by any person who is the sole head of a family or by any male eighteen years of age or over, who is a British subject or who declares his intention to become a British subject.

2. To acquire a homestead an applicant must make entry in person at the Dominion Lands Office for the district in which the land applied for is situated. At the time of entry a fee of $10.00 must be paid.

3. To earn patent for homestead, a person must reside in a habitable house upon the land for six months during each of three years.

4. Before being eligible to apply for patent, a homesteader must break (plough up) thirty acres of the homestead. It is also required that a reasonable proportion of this cultivation must be done during each homestead year.

*Canada West. The Last Best West*

*Land Titles Office, Edmonton, Alberta*

"The gummit just bet me ten bucks against a half-section that I can't stand this climate for three years."

J. M. Minifie, *Homesteader*, pp. 42-43

The head of one family, who arrived in Sifton in 1898, had barely enough money to buy a team of oxen. His homestead was ten miles away, deep in the bush. He had to chop his way through, which took him a solid week. The other family, with two small children, arrived at Selkirk in 1904; they were going to settle at Winnipeg Beach where they had a relative. They had only ten cents; this they paid to be ferried across the river. Then they took to the railroad track, the mother and father carrying their children as well as their bundles. Somehow they made it; then, says Rev. Hubicz, "they sat down on their bundles and wept." They knew no one and could not speak English; and they were unable to find their relative.

J. W. Chafe, *Extraordinary Tales from Manitoba History*, p. 140

There were Canadian and American land speculators who bought up large blocks to retail to land-hungry immigrants who poured into the "Golden West". These grants and block purchases drastically limited the choice and location of free land to the legitimate settler without limiting official inducements.

J. M. Minifie, *Homesteader*, p. 2

## FIRST SUPPLIES

A barrel of lime
100 pounds flour
50 pounds sugar
6 tubes of yeast-cakes
5 pounds Red Rose Tea
5 pounds Blue Ribbon Coffee
6 cans condensed milk
6 cans salmon
Enamel hand bowl
Baking soda
2 pitch forks
1 scoop-shovel
1 post hole spade
1 hand hammer
1 mallet
50 fence posts
2 rolls barbed wire
2 water pails
1 milk pail with sieve spout
1 keg 2½ inch nails
10 pounds 4 inch spikes
10 pound staples
Brace and bit
One axe
One hatchet
2 files
1 rasp
2 fifty foot lengths of rope
1 logging chain
1 tethering chain
2 pairs hobbles
2 halters
1 box copper rivets
6 pots
Flax burner
12 foot stove pipe
1 metal chimney pot
1 wooden barrel
1 can kerosene
1 storm lantern
2 table lamps
Carton of Eddy's matches
1 tin McDonald's pipe tobacco
1 tin Prince Albert pipe tobacco
1 bag table salt
20 pound coarse salt
1 block rock salt
pepper, spices, vinegar, nutmeg
Sack of old chum tobacco
cinnamon, cloves
2 rolls of tar paper
Shiplap, droplap, common board,
  2×4, 2×6 for a one-story shack
  14 feet by 24 feet
  1 door and hasp
4 hinges
2 horse blankets
2 coarse grey blankets
1 side bacon
1 sack oatmeal
1 broom

Minifie, *Homesteader*, p. 42-43

During the long winters, with the snow so high, we only had about six inches of window light sometimes. The stable was completely covered over. Dan kept his feed on the top of the stable, and shovelled a path at a steep angle to get the animals out; the first year, he had to drive them to Condies for water every day. If you were ever caught in a prairie blizzard, it was just too bad for you. However, I never heard of any casualties in our district, several had been lost, but safely returned.

M. G. Moorhouse, *Buffalo Horn Valley*, p. 9

But it was the loneliness which was the most oppressive for settlers, who were accustomed to living in compact villages in Slovakia or closed colonies in the United States. The interminable prairie, with scattered clumps of poplar and willow trees, covered by "buffalo grass", could not replace for many Slovak settlers, especially for women, the hilly villages. J. M. Kirschbaum, *Slovaks In Canada*, p. 82

Papa Fuhr had a map on which the agent had marked their farm, four squares west of Edmonton. Papa figured that was four miles. When the family was let off the train in the Edmonton station, he told mother and the children that he would walk out to see their farm and be back in a few hours. He was gone for two days, while the family, unable to speak the language they heard in the streets outside the station, waited with growing anxiety. Finally he came back to explain how big the country was; each square was not a mile but a township of six miles and their new farm home was twenty-four miles away not four. T. Cashman, *An Illustrated History of Western Canada*, p. 160

## Survival . . .

There were many arts by which the settlers survived. All the secrets of nature which the Ukrainian peasant had hoarded for generations, and others learned from Indians: how to dig seneca, the snake root, dry it and sell it to drug companies in the cities; the women searched for mushrooms and made soups to vary their meagre diet. Some settlers were able to buy guns and shoot wild chickens, ducks and deer. The housewife plucked the feathers and made feather beds. An abundance of rabbits supplied stews and skins for leggings, jackets and caps. All the family knew how to trap marten— they received three cents apiece from traders, and by selling a hundred, could obtain enough money for shoes. In winter, they cut cordwood—tamarac, poplar and jackpine, and hauled it on their sleds, selling it for forty-five to seventy-five cents a cord to the Icelanders, Swedes and Germans.

V. Lysenko, *Men In Sheepskin Coats*, p. 41

"Where's Gordon?" he asked his wife.

"He's upstairs lying down reading," she answered. "Isn't this some storm? It's a good thing we're all safe and sound inside."

"It sure is!" shivered Bill, as he peeled off his wet overalls and smock.

Just then there was a terrific CRASH! of thunder, and blinding lightning crackled through the air. It seemed as if the building would be shaken from its foundation. As the lightning ZINGED down, a ragged hole appeared in the ceiling above—just where Gordon's bed stood upstairs.

Dropping his sodden garments to the floor, Bill Craig bounded up the stairs, two at a time—when he reached his son, he found him—dead! The lightning had come down the stovepipe, and struck the iron bed on which the lad lay studying his homework.

M. Groom, *The Melted Years*, p. 45

The winter is the prairie farmer's holiday time, and holiday joys are very practical in kind. Now the fuel is cut, and rails and fence posts cut and hauled. Hay and grain are drawn to town and elevator, and stock must be fed, watered and "rounded."

*Home Life of Women In Western Canada*, p. 71

Within two decades, a single year's crop from only one of these Prairie Provinces equalled more gold in value than ever came out of the Klondike.

V. Lysenko, *Men In Sheepskin Coats*, p. 10

## Hotel Iceland

Gimli, Manitoba
March 12th, 1908

To the Commissioner of Immigration, Winnipeg

Dear Sir:

In travelling through Townships 19, 20, and 21, Ranges 2 and 3 E, I find that there is great destitution among the foreign settlers in that locality in several homes which I have visited. I have found places where people were almost on the verge of starvation, having been two or three days without bread or flour to make it. Immediate relief is necessary as they live in places where there are no roads and no chance to get anything in after the roads break up, until freezing up next winter.

Hoping you will give this your immediate attention,

I remain,
Yours
John Lusted
Forest Ranger

Public Archives of Canada

# A DREAM COME TRUE?

Breakfast at 6 a.m.; lunch in the field at 10 o'clock; dinner at the farm house at 12:30; at 4 p.m. a "snack in the field" consisting of buttered bread, cold meat, cheese, pie, cake; and hot coffee, borne in the great kettle and poured by the farm mistress, who bears away the emptied platters, only to see them well replenished at 6 p.m., when the horn sounds for supper.

*Home Life of Women In Western Canada*, p. 6

## THE CITY OF SASKATOON

### Province of Saskatchewan

January 20, 1909

G.E. McCraney, M.P.
House of Commons
Ottawa, Ontario

Dear Sir:

I am instructed by the Council of the Corporation of the City of Saskatoon to advise you that John Lang, homesteader, residing on the S.E. 36-35-6- Ws 3rd, disappeared on December 1st, 1908, his wife was sick and he came into town to get some medicine, and after leaving the City he has not been seen since, supposition being that he was frozen to death.

He left a wife and seven children ranging from two months to nine years old in very destitute circumstances. The family being in such a deplorable condition, it was thought advisable to bring them into the City, and they were placed in Emigration Hall.

The mother died of pneumonia on January 11th 1909, thus leaving the seven children orphans, and being cared for by the City. We have communicated with her people in Scotland, but as yet have received no reply.

The City Council have asked me to take this matter up with you to ascertain what would be in the best steps to take regarding the taking care of the children.

Thanking you in anticipation of your attention to this matter.

I am yours truly,
J.H. Trusdale,
City Clerk

Public Archives of Canada

Spring opens up in March. The routine of farm life is usually: At six o'clock breakfast is on the table. The menfolk are, since five o'clock, out in the barns turning out the cattle to water—milking the cows and turning the foaming rich white fluid into the separator, which gives from one spout cream for home and butter-making use, and from another milk to fatten calves and pigs for market. After the stables are cleaned, the men breakfast, and then it is off to the fields, where ploughing, harrowing and rolling the soil goes on, followed by seeding; all of which is done by machinery under skilled orders.     *Home Life of Women In Western Canada*, p. 4

"A wedge of limestone judged to weigh 71 million metric tons and measuring about 390 metres from top to bottom, and 720 metres in width, suddenly dropped from the side of the mountain."     J. M. Kirschbaum, *Slovaks In Canada*, p. 72

Rust is a fungus disease that seriously reduces the yield of any grain it attacks. Serious crop damage was caused on the prairies by a heavy attack in 1896 and another in 1904 which was widely reported to have "robbed farmers (both American and Canadian) of 100,000,000 bushels of wheat."

J. M. Minifie, *Homesteader*, p. 5

In my commissary the labourers could buy bacon, flour and canned goods of tolerable quality, but for prices that New York clubs would be ashamed to ask. Those who didn't like it could get out (at their own expense), for there was a never-ending stream of new serfs, shanghaied by the mass procurement agencies of the East."     *Friends In Need*, p. 47

*The day after the Frank Slide, Alberta, 1903*

"The mass (flew) with terrific speed across the valley for a distance of almost two miles.... It covered.... 1292.8 hectares (3,200 acres) to a depth of 30 metres."     J. M. Kirschbaum, *Slovaks In Canada*, p. 72

1899

Tragic Trek of Fifty-five Ukrainian Children, in May. 55 children and two adults die in the settlement trek and tents at Lake Patterson, Manitoba, from disease and mostly the freezing cold. In 1941 a monument marking the 50th anniversary of Ukrainian settlement was erected on the site where the original tents stood.     A. S. Gregorovich, *Chronology of Ukrainian Canadian History*, p. 12

# PRAIRIE COMMUNITY LIFE

## THE WOMANS QUIET HOUR
### By E.C.H.

One room at a time should be the motto of every housewife in spring cleaning and if, as will happen among many of the new settlers, there is but one, or at most two rooms, than take two or even three days for the necessary turning out.

Naptha soap, made by the Royal Crown Co., Limited, Winnipeg, if you can get it, is one of the best and easiest soaps with which to wash blankets, and I hope there are not many homes in our great Canadian West without a wringer. With these two things, blanket washing is greatly simplified.

A man should be almost as much ashamed to have his wife go without a wringer and washing machine as he would be to have her go without shoes.

*Western Home Monthly*, May 1907, p. 30

Children have abounding health, and old people appear to renew their youth; the only disease I have observed at all troublesome is rheumatism, and there are special points in the West, such as Banff, in Alberta, where this trouble is treated with success.

*Home Life of Women in Western Canada, p. 36*

*Interior of John Beam's ranch house, north of Cochrane, Alberta*

In time a church was built. The seats were planks laid on logs and later four kitchen chairs which Dad obtained at cost price. Dr. Thurlow Fraser, then minister at Portage la Prairie, opened and dedicated this church in August 1904. The newly organized Ladies' Aid put on concerts and suppers to pay for the chairs and also for bracket lamps. These church concerts and suppers were really something. I have often heard mother tell of how she personally made up a bushel of potatoes into salad and of how she would make as many as 30 lemon pies. The men used to flock in from the outlying lumber camps and a good many landseekers also used to come.

H. Robertson, *Salt of the Earth*, p. 124

*Thresher's dinner on Siebrasse farm, 1913*

My Dad often said "This is the finest place in the world to raise a family in. The young folk are all so decent and clean minded. When a bunch of boys got together, you never heard them belittle girls. When we left Ontario, all settled their disagreements at the next dance, like the old song, "Many a heart is broken, after the ball". We would hear men say, "I'll get him at the next dance". Many a fight took place there, when everyone was dressed in his best and should be having a good time. We seldom saw this behavior on the prairie.

M. G. Moorhouse, *Buffalo Horn Valley*, p. 27

*Three happy settlers*

Mr. Cooper, who was batching for a few winter months, would run out of tobacco so many times, and get lost while trying to locate a loan. When a rap come to a door about 3 a.m., someone would yell, "Is that you, Cooper?" It wouldn't do to come to our place, Dad didn't smoke. He was welcome to anything else he might need. Every one helped everyone else out. Dad had the only sleigh in the country, and he never knew where it was.

M. G. Moorhouse, *Buffalo Horn Valley*, p. 9

We had a young Irish youth there one night, and he was fascinated by the stories and tried hard not to believe them. But he left the house, looking quite white, and told us afterwards he had run the whole four miles home.

M. G. Moorhouse, *Buffalo Horn Valley*, p. 27

Interior of home, Moose Jaw, Saskatchewan

Doukhobor women

## Women at work

But to come home again, let us give heed to the household question, that question which is with us all, and always with us. I have seen women in England nearly worn out with their servant-worries, their kitchen-ranges, and their complicated household arrangements. I would not change places with them for any consideration, even to have dinner in six courses every evening. Here we enjoy the luxury of one servant in the house, an able-bodied cook, and I never heard him complain that his cooking-stove had "gone back on him"; nor if he did, should I lie awake at night thinking about it. I made the usual mistake of bringing out a maid from home; but when in course of time the mistake rectified itself, and she went the way of all womankind in the West, I took to the broom and duster, and was surprised to find what a calmness descended on my spirit with release from the task of supervision. An average of two hours' housework a day, and the trouble of mending one's own clothes, is not much to pay for all the joys of liberty. L. G. Thomas, *The Prairie West to 1905*, p. 301

## A SONG TO THE OLD SHACK

*I love it. I love it. And who shall dare*
*To chide me for loving the old shack there.*
*It has sheltered us all from wet and cold.*
*No money can buy it. It cannot be sold.*

*I've climbed it. I've climbed it. And all shall share*
*The trembling uncertainty of that rickety stair.*
*But it has carried us up to the regions above*
*Where we dreamed of our fortunes, our lands and our love.*

*I've scrubbed it. I've scrubbed it, that dirty old shack*
*And finished so oft with a kink in my back.*
*I've slivered my fingers on the rotten old floor*
*And wondered at night why my knees were so sore.*

*I've trimmed it and decked it, that crooked old shack,*
*I've whitewashed and painted and used some shellac,*
*I've papered and draped it with cretonne and such*
*And when I get there it doesn't look much.*

*But I love it, I love it, that dear old shack,*
*Wherever I wander I always come back,*
*With a warm thought in my heart for the joy and the pride*
*One always feels for one's own fireside.*

Written by Annabel Rainforth in 1905 or 1906

*Wagon Trails To Hard Top*, p. 238

"How do I like the social side of prairie life? Immensely. For pure joy of informality in social life Western Canada stands away ahead of all the places I know. We visit each other and have our social enjoyments quite like other people, and what I like best about the country is the happy-hearted hospitality with which strangers are met on coming here. Life in Western Canada is delightful. *Women's Work In Western Canada*, p. 63

# CITIES

### POPULATION

|  | 1891 | 1901 | 1911 |
|---|---|---|---|
| Halifax | 38,437 | 40,832 | 46,619 |
| Quebec City | 63,090 | 68,840 | 78,710 |
| Montreal | 256,723 | 328,172 | 490,504 |
| Toronto | 181,215 | 209,892 | 381,833 |
| Ottawa | 44,154 | 59,928 | 87,062 |
| Winnipeg | 25,639 | 42,340 | 136,035 |
| Regina | – – | 2,249 | 30,213 |
| Edmonton | – – | 4,176 | 31,064 |
| Calgary | 3,876 | 4,392 | 43,704 |
| Vancouver | 13,709 | 29,432 | 120,847 |

Census of Canada, 1931

Cobalt, Ontario

## ⚡ HEAVY MORTALITY AMONG INFANTS

There was considerable discussion among a number of aldermen at the City Hall to-day over the report, in the Star last night, that over one hundred children had died in the city last week.

The feeling of the aldermen was that something ought to be done immediately to remedy such an alarming state of affairs.

The medical health officer, Dr. Laberge, said to-day that in addition to the deaths among infants, due to improper care of young mothers, infant mortality was greatly increased on account of the large number of privy pits in the city.

*Montreal Star, 5 July 1904, p. 1*

### ⚡ TYPHOID IN THE SUBURBS

Typhoid is now epidemic in Westmount, St. Henri and St. Cunnegonde. The one thing which these municipalities have in common, which is not shared by Montreal, is the water supply, the character of which has been severely criticised during the last two years. The fact indicated at least a strong probability that the typhoid is due to contaminated water.

*Montreal Star, 5 Jan. 1904, p. 46*

Saskatoon, Saskatchewan

Moose Jaw, Saskatchewan

# SWEPT BY FIERCE FLAMES!

Ottawa 1900
Toronto 1904
South Porcupine 1911

Toronto, Ontario

### ONTARIO LEGISLATION RESPECTING MOTOR VEHICLES
#### *Toronto 1905*

1. Every person in control of a motor vehicle, whenever approaching a vehicle drawn by horse or horses, shall exercise precaution to prevent the frightening of such horse or horses . . . shall not approach or pass such a vehicle at a greater speed than seven miles per hour.

2. A person in charge of a motor vehicle or a vehicle drawn by horses who meets another vehicle shall turn right from the centre of the road allowing the vehicle so met one-half of the road.

3. No motor vehicle shall be run within any city, town or incorporated village at a greater speed than 10 miles an hour or outside of a city at a greater speed than 15 miles an hour.

4. Every motor vehicle shall be equipped with a proper bell, gong or horn and shall carry in front a lighted lamp.

5. In case a person in a motor vehicle overtakes any motor vehicle, vehicle or bicycle said person shall give to the person audible warning of his approach before attempting to pass.

6. In case a person in charge of a vehicle or horse travelling is through drunkenness unable to drive or ride with safety he shall incur the penalty of $1 – $20.

7. Every person travelling upon a highway with a sleigh, sled or cariole drawn by horse or mule, shall have at least two bells attached to the harness.

Ontario Archives

*Fire on Front Street, Toronto, Ontario*

*Québec City, Québec*

# LIVING IN THE CITY...

Their agent had intended to send them to the West; but they were told by fellow settlers that the West was a barren windswept waste. In desperation, their agent contacted one August Peterson who had taken up a homestead in the Township of Bucke, just a few weeks before. (Peterson Lake, west of Cobalt, bears his name).

Peterson wrote their agent in glowing terms, urging them by all means to come North.

"It's just like Sweden here," he wrote . . .          M. Groom, *The Melted Years*, p. 23

---

**WANTED YOUNG WOMAN OF 20**

Mayville, Alta., March 24, 1907.

Editor.—Your correspondence columns are immense. I am in a part of the country where young ladies are scarce. My trouble, however, is that I am very reserved and am not likely to make many lady friends around here for two reasons: 1, that the girls are either married or are children, 2, I do not care sufficiently for dances. Of course the ladies will say what a selfish fellow. I am not a dancer and am not looking for a feed; and the inducements are not sufficient to tempt me out of a frosty night. I do not live in the wilderness and am not a "batcher" but a "bachelor." If any young woman of my own age (20) cares to correspond with me please give her my address.

"Stub L"

*Western Home Monthly*, May 1907, p. 12

The Massey home in Toronto, 1898

---

**Marriage Licenses.**

MARRIAGE LICENSES AT SHUFF'S Drug Store, 540 Dundas street east, corner William. Trolley cars pass the door. No witnesses required.

MARRIAGE LICENSES ISSUED—OFFICE Adkins Jewelry Store, East London. No witnesses required.

WM. H. WESTON, ISSUER OF MARRIAGE licenses, 64 Stanley street. No witnesses required.

LICENSES ISSUED BY THOS. GILLEAN Jeweler, 602 Richmond street.

*London Advertiser*, 14 Dec. 1898, p. 3

**THE SCHOOL FOR YOUNG LADIES,**
Conducted by
**Miss Symmers and Miss Smith,**
will re-open on Monday, 11th January
916 Sherbrooke Street          3 6

*Montreal Star*, 5 Jan. 1904, p. 4

*A Winnipeg garden party*

It is worthy of note that during the past year all the typhoid occurring in the city was what is sometimes called the residual type, that is, it was not due to infection carried by water or milk . . . We are unable to recall any year in the past decade in which we did not have at least one well-marked outbreak, due to infection of a milk route . . . We cannot but conclude that the increased vigilance which has been exercised over the milk supply, particularly with regard to illness at dairies, has had some effect.

J. S. Woodsworth, *My Neighbour,* p. 119

The young couple shopped around the crowded streets of Cobalt for a few hours. Woolworth's 15¢ store was an attraction for Sadie, from there they picked up the funny-papers and the "Cobalt Nugget" at Stadleman's Book Store. Bob treated his brand new wife to a dish of Eplett's ice-cream in the "Minerva Tea-Room". From there the pair went up Lang Street where Bob had his watch repaired in Belchum's Jewellery Shop.

They topped the day off by going to the movies at the Bijoux Theatre on Lang Street. It was quite late when finally they went down to the station to catch the streetcar back to their new home.

M. Groom, *The Melted Years,* pp. 83-84

# LIVING IN THE CITY...

*Alleyway in Montreal*

## Labourers' Houses...

The houses of common labourers were of the most primitive character, one storey high, usually containing one small window, and often but one small pane of glass. The material used in construction is the commonest rough lumber with no attempt at architectural design or taste, simply thrown together as if intended for but temporary occupation, somewhat resembling a railroad or lumberman's camp, and certainly no improvement upon either. Entering a long, dark, narrow alleyway, our guide leading the way by striking a match at intervals, stumbling over a muddy, uneven walk, the faint glimmer of a light appears in the distance, emanating from the small, dirty window, casting a yellow glow upon the smoky and soot-covered walls on the opposite side of the alley, revealing a net-work of small, partly covered passageways leading in all directions through this human beehive. Approaching an entrance, our guide at length located the latch, and unannounced, rudely pushes open the door. We enter a small 10 × 10 foot room without a ceiling.

C. H. Young and H. R. Y. Reid, *The Japanese Canadians*, p. 212

Our work is all among the poor, and only yesterday one of our workers went to a home where father, mother and five children were living in two rooms. One child was tubercular. They were sleeping four in one bed, and the sick child on a couch. These children sleep in the living-room. There was another case where a child was born in one of these homes. The mother was in an advanced stage of tuberculosis and father, mother and four children slept in a room 10 ft. × 12 ft. The kitchen was a mite of a place only large enough for a stove, table and chairs. These people living in this huddled condition and with no precaution whatever taken against this disease, you can imagine what chances these children have.

J. S. Woodsworth, *My Neighbour*, pp. 137-138

*Interior of a Macedonian boarding house, Toronto, 1913*

## A Chinese Boarding House

Ascending a narrow stairway we enter what had apparently once been a large room, some 18 × 30 feet with a 10 foot ceiling, but which had an additional floor, occupying a position nearly midway between the floor and the ceiling, thus making two stories out of one. The lower floor was divided off into small rooms reached by a number of narrow hallways, each room containing three low bunks covered with a Chinese mat. In many cases a double tier of these bunks was observed. The covering, in a moderately clean condition, consists of a mat and one or two quilts. The second or upper floor was reached by a short stairway. Here no attempt seems to have been made at a division of space, at least by partitioning, but at intervals a small mat is spread out on the floor with some regularity, by which each individual is enabled to locate his own particular claim. In many cases even a third floor exists, reached usually by a narrow rickety stairway, into which the occupant crawls upon his hands and knees. Here we found an almost entire absence of light and ventilation, the occupants using a small smoky, open lamp, to discover their respective locations, the fumes from which add to the discomfort of the surroundings.

C. H. Young and H. R. Y. Reid,
*The Japanese Canadians*, p. 212

# ANOTHER LOOK

But with the growth of our cities, the influx of foreign immigrants, and the development of our industrial life we have now large areas known as undesirable residential districts—in some instances bad enough to be called slums. Here we find the waste of society—those who have not 'made good', the unfortunate, the depraved. Here are those who have had to remain at the bottom—the unskilled workers of all kinds. Here too settle, at first, the newcomers who must start at the bottom. And so to complicate an already difficult problem we have our 'foreign colonies'—our Ghettos, Little Italys, Colored Blocks and Chinatowns, and whole foreign wards with their mixed population from Southeastern Europe.

J. S. Woodsworth, *My Neighbour*, p. 104

A small room at the back, very crowded, with double bed, small stove and table. The air was very, very bad and both door and window were kept tightly closed. Father was out looking for work. The mother was out washing. The stove was dirty and piled up with dirty pots and kettles. The table showed signs of breakfast—dirty granite dishes and spoons, two whiskey bottles and part of a loaf of bread from which the cat was now having breakfast. The bed was like all the beds in this class of home—mattress covered by an old grey blanket, two big, dirty-looking pillows and some old clothes. This was the children's playground, for there was no floor space uncovered. Under the bed we noticed some cooking utensils, white-wash brush, an axe, spade, a dozen or more empty bottles, some clothing and a sack of bread.

J. S. Woodsworth, *My Neighbour*, p. 68

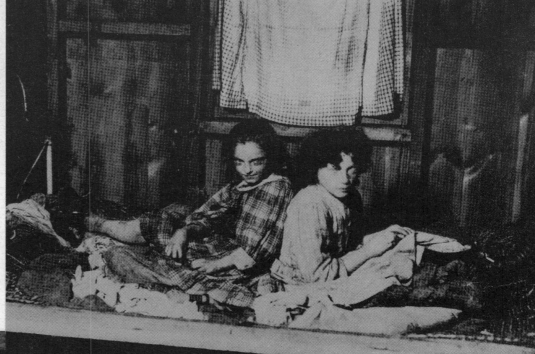

Pneumonia is said to flourish among ill-fed, ill-clothed, badly-nourished population, especially when crowded together amid insanitary surrounding, with an insufficient supply of pure air and sunshine.

J. S. Woodsworth, *My Neighbour*, p. 120

Dear Mother and Father:

Remember we thought that Canada must be a land of farms and wheat fields, this being the impression we had from the posters back home? It is true that there are many farms but there are also many large towns and I am living in Edmonton. This town has many industries and is a busy place as farmers from the surrounding area come here to buy supplies.

I have found steady employment in a warehouse and spend my days loading and unloading boxes. I am living in a home in one of the poorer parts of the city. Many Europeans live here also, and while we are crowded and shabby, we live in harmony. Soon I hope to have put aside enough money to find more suitable lodgings. While I do not wish to take up farming, I am looking for different work. Please do not worry about me as I am healthy. I get a little tired sometimes, but that is just the job.

Your loving son,
Joseph

# PEOPLE AT WORK

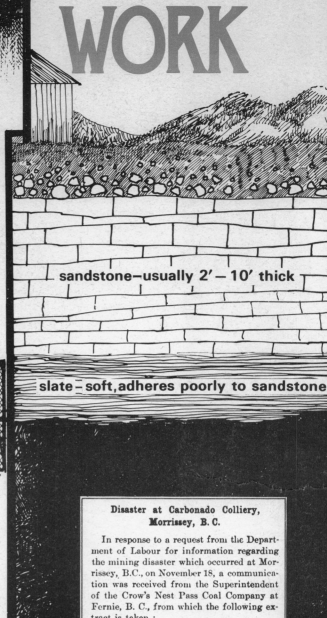

A hacking cough tugs at his chest,
His eyes swell up, and his face turns blacker than night,
And from his heart swells a sea of grief;
Then ask, brother, which is the greatest suffering —
In the old world or the new?

*V. Lysenko, Men in Sheepskin Coats, p. 92*

sandstone—usually 2' – 10' thick

slate – soft, adheres poorly to sandstone

*Coal miners at work in Cape Breton, 1906*

### Disaster at Carbonado Colliery, Morrissey, B. C.

In response to a request from the Department of Labour for information regarding the mining disaster which occurred at Morrissey, B.C., on November 18, a communication was received from the Superintendent of the Crow's Nest Pass Coal Company at Fernie, B. C., from which the following extract is taken :

' At 11.50 on that day an outburst of gas took place in the face of one of the main levels in No. 1 Mine, Carbonado Colliery. Owing to the outburst giving very little warning, all the men in the mine, numbering fourteen, were suffocated by the gas. About 30 minutes before the outburst took place the overman of that mine had been in all the working places in the mine, as well as in the place where the outburst occurred and found everything in normal condition. The men had evidently received some little warning, as they were all found in the main level, some four or five hundred feet from the face, and heading out towards the mouth of the mine. They were carrying their clothes and lunch baskets with them, and were evidently making their escape when the gas overtook them.

*Labour Gazette, Dec. 1904, p. 639*

### NOTICE TO EMPLOYEES

Circular of the Nova Scotia Steel Company respecting Accidents.

With a view to the prevention of accidents among its employees, the Nova Scotia Steel Company recently issued the following circular: –

To all concerned:

We have had so many accidents in and about our collieries during the past few weeks, that we take this means of appealing to our officers and men on this important subject.

We expect that our officers are doing everything in their power to carry out the special rules and mining law as regards accidents and we also expect that they are insisting upon the workmen doing the same.

Our workmen would help us very much if they would call the attention of the officer in charge to any dangerous practice or any source of danger, or anything or practice that might cause an accident.

While we expect our officers to report any workmen that violate the mining law or special rules, we would go further and ask our workmen to report to the manager any violation of the law or any oversight of a violation on the part of any of our officers.

If our men would only observe some of the following dont's a great many accidents might be avoided: – Don't rush hurriedly back to see the result of your shot; don't get down and mine under a block of coal unless securely spragged; don't work under bad or suspicious roof; don't travel any other road but the travelling road provided; don't ride on trips when riding is forbidden; don't violate any of the rules or laws which have been prepared to protect you in your hazardous occupation, and don't forget that all these laws and rules have been prepared for your own protection, and don't expect any lawmaker or company can protect you if you neglect to do so yourself.

Our laws are many and good – but they are no good and not worth the paper they are written on, unless the miner gives them his hearty and intelligent co-operation.

*Labour Gazette, July 1904, p. 97*

*Sewer construction workers in Toronto*

The commissioners noted one case of three men who subsisted for a whole day on one onion. Some men leaving one camp were refused a pinch of salt they requested to salt fish they hoped to catch with a fish hook given to them by one of their co-workers. They had hoped to live on fish during a 150 mile walk from the camp to Fort MacLeod.

Two Armenians who did not like the food at their camp (it was against their customs to eat some that was served) were allowed to board themselves. They were happy to find they could buy supplies from the CPR cheaper than from their contractor's camp. When they made the mistake of making this known, they were promptly fired. J. M. Kirschbaum, *Slovaks in Canada*, p. 74

## "40 DIE IN EXPLOSION AS CPR LEVELS HILL"

The Telegraph of February 8, 1910, reported "an army of 4,027 slain and 13,368 injured on the CPR and GTR in deaths in twenty years. It is cheaper," noted the newspaper, "to pay for a certain number of deaths than put the service on a safety basis." *Friends in Need*, p. 49

My friend cannot read or write English and was told by the railway contractor that he would only be required to clear bush so he signed a work contract. Now he has been told he must pay for blankets and work as a pick and shovel man. When he complained the R.C.M.P. was called in and the officer told him if he could prove he was brought here under false pretenses, he would be discharged from his contract.

*—a railway construction worker*

*Canadian Pacific car wreck, 1910*

## Work and Wages Waiting in Canada for All Who Seek Them.

How a Young Englishman, Without Money or Friends, Can Earn His Living Here in a Dozen Different Ways if He Is Willing to Do It. . . . . . .

A Convincing Reply to the Wail of Discontented Immigrants That There Is No Work to Be Obtained in Canada by an Immigrant Who Found Lots of It. . .

LETTER No. 1.

In most of these complaints regarding the conditions of life in the Land of the Maple Leaf, we find stress is laid upon the fact that "work could not be got." and it is my intention in these articles to show by my own personal experience that work can be got by any man willing to take it—that there is no need for any man to go idle or hungry in this land of plenty, and that the responsibility of failure rests solely and entirely upon a man's own shoulders and not upon the conditions of labour in the country.

*Montreal Star, 20 Aug. 1904, p. 5*

### COTTON MILLS STRIKE

**The Five Hundred Employees of a Hamilton Firm Walk Out.**

Hamilton, May 6.—The Imperial Cotton Company shut down yesterday as the result of a strike, affecting between four and five hundred employees. A general increase of ten per cent was made by the company during the last wave of prosperity. Two years ago, when the business depression was felt, five per cent was cut off, and this was followed later by another reduction of a similar amount. Two weeks ago the employees demanded that the ten per cent be restored. The company refused, so the employees walked out in a body.

The superintendent says the company is willing to grant the ten per cent as soon as conditions warrant it. He declares that on account of the high price of cotton the cotton manufacturers of the country are in worse shape than they have been for years. The mill has been running full time with its usual staff, while other mills have been working short hours with reduced staffs.

*London Advertiser, 6 May 1910, p. 6*

*Interior of clothing factory, London, Ontario*

### WAGES IN A NEW WESTMINSTER CANNERY 1897 – 1900

Avg. wages per month paid to:

| CHINESE | | WHITES |
|---|---|---|
| $38.54 | 1897 | $79.58 |
| $37.58 | 1898 | $75.71 |
| $39.39 | 1899 | $77.21 |
| $40.15 | 1900 | $80.91 |

| PAY TO THE ORDER OF … | BRICKLAYERS | | CARPENTERS | | ELECTRICIANS | | PAINTERS | | COMMON LABOURERS IN FACTORIES | |
|---|---|---|---|---|---|---|---|---|---|---|
| LOCATION | Wages Per Hour | Hours Per week | Wages Per Hour | Hours Per week | Wages Per Hour | Hours Per week | Wages Per Hour | Hours Per week | Wages Per Hour | Hours Per week |
| HALIFAX | .40 | 54 | .30 | 54 | .25 | 54 | .25 | 54 | .15 | 54 |
| ST. JOHN | .45 | 54 | .27 | 54 | .25 | 54 | .27 | 54 | ... | ... |
| QUEBEC | .45 | 54 | .27 | 54 | .22 | 60 | .25 | 54 | ... | ... |
| HAMILTON | .50 | 44 | .37 | 44 | .30 | 54 | .30 | 50 | .17 | 59 |
| WINNIPEG | .60 | 53 | .45 | 50/54 | .40 | 48/54 | .30/.40 | 53 | .25 | 55 |
| REGINA | .60 | 54 | .35 | 59 | .35 | 54 | .30 | 60 | ... | ... |
| EDMONTON | .60 | 48 | .43 | 48 | .40 | 48 | .45 | 48 | .25 | 58 |
| VICTORIA | .70 | 44 | .50 | 44 | .56 | 44 | .43 | 44 | .17 | 55 |

*Dep't. of Labour. Wages and Hours of Labour in Canada*

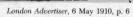

*Swift's Packing Company, Edmonton, Alberta, 1910*

### TABLE OF FATAL INDUSTRIAL ACCIDENTS DURING 1904.

| Trade or Industry. | Jan. | Feb. | Mar. | April. | May. | June | July. | Aug. | Sept. | Oct. | Nov. | Dec. | Total. |
|---|---|---|---|---|---|---|---|---|---|---|---|---|---|
| Agriculture | 7 | 8 | 6 | 3 | 11 | 12 | 17 | 18 | 11 | 4 | 10 | 3 | 110 |
| Fishing and hunting | 2 | | | 1 | 2 | 4 | 2 | | 5 | | | | 16 |
| Lumbering | 5 | 8 | 5 | 2 | 12 | 12 | 6 | 6 | 1 | 4 | 7 | 1 | 69 |
| Mining | 16 | 9 | 8 | 11 | 6 | 5 | 4 | 14 | 6 | 7 | 18 | 2 | 106 |
| Building trades | 2 | 1 | 3 | 1 | 6 | 5 | 1 | 8 | 2 | 5 | 8 | 1 | 43 |
| Metal trades | 11 | 5 | 11 | 7 | 3 | 5 | 4 | 6 | 7 | 2 | 8 | 4 | 73 |
| Woodworking trades | 1 | | 2 | 1 | 2 | 2 | | | | 1 | 1 | 2 | 12 |
| Printing trades | | | | | | | | | | | | | |
| Clothing trades | 1 | | | | 2 | | | | | | | | 3 |
| Textile trades | | | 1 | 1 | | | | | | | 2 | | 4 |
| Food and tobacco preparation | 2 | | | 1 | 1 | | | | | | | 2 | 6 |
| Leather trades | | | | | | 1 | | | | 1 | | | 2 |
| Railway service | 21 | 27 | 19 | 26 | 20 | 18 | 26 | 22 | 31 | 26 | 20 | 17 | 278 |
| General transport | 5 | 5 | 1 | 4 | 16 | 9 | 11 | 14 | 13 | 10 | 12 | 4 | 104 |
| Miscellaneous trades | 5 | 6 | | 4 | 2 | 3 | 6 | 3 | 1 | 2 | 7 | 4 | 43 |
| Unskilled labour | | 2 | 3 | | | 6 | 2 | 5 | 3 | 4 | 2 | 3 | 30 |
| Total | 78 | 71 | 59 | 62 | 84 | 81 | 79 | 96 | 80 | 65 | 96 | 43 | 894 |

*Labour Gazette, Jan. 1905, p. 742*

Wages were fixed at all camps, and ranged from $1.50 a day (27½ day month) for labourers, to $26.00 a month for axemen. A week's board consumed $4.00 and transportation from McLeod to the camp $2.00 to $7.00 irrespective of the fact whether they rode on the wagons or walked beside them. The workers further paid 50 cents a month medical fees and 25 cents a month to receive mail. A man who worked at $1.50 a day would have earned after a year's employment an average of $387.00. However, his total expenses while on the job amounted to $381.60. This left the labourer with a profit of $5.40 for his year's effort. It was estimated that 2,000 were handled in this way.

J. M. Kirschbaum, *Slovaks in Canada*, p. 73

*Rotary plough clears track in the Selkirks*

## "HOSTILITY TO ORIENTAL LABOUR GROWS"

# BUILDING THE RAILWAY

What I couldn't swallow was the ruthless, brazen robbery of the ignorant Ukrainians. As timekeeper in charge of sales and books, I was agent for the robbers. True enough, the lowliest of labourers got three dollars a day, a bunk with a vermin-infested blanket and pillow and free grub. But the food doled out in meagre rations was barely edible.

V. Lysenko, *Men in Sheepskin Coats*, p. 56

*Lauder, Manitoba*

### RAILWAY SERVICE.

| Causes of Accidents. | Killed. | Injured. |
|---|---|---|
| Struck by engines, etc. | 53 | 35 |
| Injured in collisions | 33 | 77 |
| Derailing of engines, cars, etc | 18 | 24 |
| Injured when coupling | 12 | 24 |
| Falling from trains and cars | 22 | 49 |
| Falling from trains and run over | 26 | 3 |
| Foot catching in frogs, etc., and run over | 5 | 5 |
| Run over by trains, etc., in other ways | 47 | 23 |
| Injured by boiler explosions | 3 | 5 |
| Injured by blasting, dynamite, etc | 20 | 12 |
| Suffocated by coal gas | 6 | 1 |
| Crushed between cars, engines, etc. | 10 | 16 |
| Crushed in roundhouses and shops | 2 | 5 |
| Striking objects when on moving trains | 1 | 2 |
| Striking objects when on electric car. | .. | 2 |
| Injured by falling snow and rock | 4 | .. |
| Injured by electric shock | 2 | .. |
| Struck by falling freight | 1 | 8 |
| Struck by falling metal | .. | 5 |
| Falling from ladders | .. | 2 |
| Falling in other ways | 4 | 13 |
| Injured by tools | .. | 2 |
| Injured by a saw | .. | 1 |
| Injured by machinery, belting, etc. | .. | 1 |
| Injured by an elevator | .. | 1 |
| Unclassified | 4 | 29 |

*Labour Gazette*, Jan. 1905, p. 745

# CURES

*General Hospital, Regina, 1900*

## THE DOUKHOBORS

**Vaccinated and Disinfected — No Fresh Case of Smallpox Reported**

Halifax, N.S. Jan. 30. — No illness has appeared among the Doukhobors now at the quarantine since their arrival, and the health officials feel confident that there will be no reappearance of smallpox. The work of vaccination and disinfection has been in progress constantly since Saturday morning.

*London Advertiser, 30 Jan. 1898, p. 6*

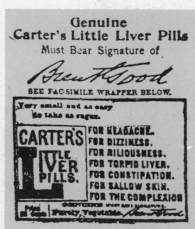
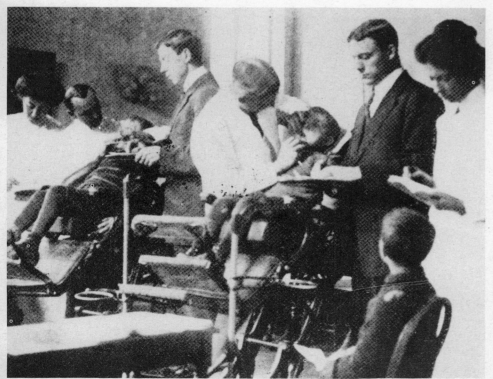

*Free dental clinic in a public school, c. 1911*

## OCCUPATION, AGE, BIRTH PLACE, RESIDENCE OF PERSONS CONVICTED OF OFFENSES 1901 – 1912

| | 1901 | 1903 | 1905 | 1907 | 1909 | 1911 |
|---|---|---|---|---|---|---|
| **Occupations:** | | | | | | |
| Agricultural | 198 | 248 | 281 | 244 | 590 | 545 |
| Commercial | 709 | 810 | 1,061 | 913 | 1,296 | 1,601 |
| Domestic | 173 | 193 | 216 | 569 | 524 | 654 |
| Industrial | 652 | 634 | 1,007 | 905 | 1,067 | 887 |
| Professional | 45 | 42 | 48 | 77 | 98 | 112 |
| Labourer | 2,127 | 2,464 | 3,006 | 2,969 | 4,229 | 4,767 |
| Not given | 1,730 | 2,130 | 2,005 | 3,433 | 3,645 | 4,061 |
| **Ages** | | | | | | |
| Under 16 years | 1,017 | 1,038 | 800 | 1.004 | 1,150 | 1,439 |
| 16 years and under 21 | 882 | 991 | 1,336 | 1,280 | 1,525 | 1,640 |
| 21 years and under 40 | 2,391 | 2,744 | 3,586 | 3,708 | 5,050 | 5,795 |
| 40 years and over | 806 | 849 | 935 | 1,048 | 1,424 | 1,562 |
| Not given | 538 | 899 | 967 | 2,069 | 2,300 | 2,191 |
| **Birth places:** | | | | | | |
| England and Wales | 358 | 377 | 579 | 732 | 944 | 1,746 |
| Ireland | 165 | 167 | 165 | 229 | 247 | 302 |
| Scotland | 61 | 126 | 104 | 200 | 241 | 365 |
| Canada | 4,056 | 4,306 | 4,694 | 4,675 | 6,106 | 6,376 |
| Other British possessions | 12 | 23 | 26 | 2 | 32 | 16 |
| United States | 231 | 309 | 360 | 436 | 514 | 734 |
| Other foreign countries | 259 | 447 | 844 | 880 | 1,281 | 1,547 |
| Not given | 492 | 766 | 852 | 1,956 | 2,084 | 2,041 |
| **Residence:** | | | | | | |
| Cities and towns | 4,220 | 4,729 | 5,785 | 6,173 | 7,916 | 9,610 |
| Rural districts | 961 | 1,058 | 1,084 | 1,040 | 1,593 | 1,459 |
| Not given | 453 | 734 | 755 | 1,897 | 1,940 | 1,558 |

*Canada Year Book, 1906, pp. 484-485, 1913, p. 621*

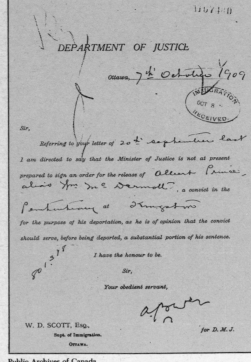

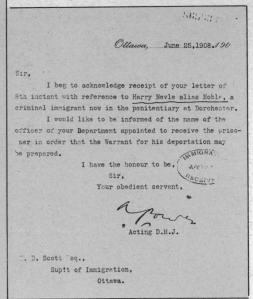

Public Archives of Canada

# CRIME AND

*North West Mounted Police, "K"*

I am informed that you have commenced squatting on land within the lease of Mr. J. R. Craig, which is valuable for hay and watering purposes; if this information is correct it would be in your own interest to desist from this attempt. If within Mr. Craig's lease, he can eject you at any time and if the land is valuable for stock-watering purposes, the Government will certainly do so.    L. G. Thomas, *The Prairie West*, p. 285

### LASHED AS A WARNING
#### Winnipeg Sandbaggers Get Severe Punishment

Winnipeg, March 14—At the Winnipeg assizes yesterday Judge Richardson sentenced John Sandscock, the "hold-up" man, to fifteen years imprisonment and seventy-five lashes and McDonald who assisted him in the work got ten years and twenty-five lashes.

*Edmonton Journal, 14 Mar. 1905, p. 1*

---

*Halifax police, 1901*

## CONVICTIONS FOR INDICTABLE OFFENCES IN THE DOMINION 1901 – 1905

| Indictable offences | 1901 | | 1902 | | 1903 | | 1904 | | 1905 | |
|---|---|---|---|---|---|---|---|---|---|---|
| | M | F | M | F | M | F | M | F | M | F |
| Arson | 20 | 1 | 23 | 1 | 32 | 1 | 34 | 1 | 29 | — |
| Assault, aggravated | 223 | 6 | 196 | 10 | 300 | 15 | 243 | 15 | 245 | 7 |
| Assault and battery | 198 | 9 | 401 | 15 | 352 | 13 | 416 | 25 | 385 | 14 |
| Assault on a peace officer | 334 | 18 | 325 | 14 | 418 | 28 | 404 | 23 | 454 | 17 |
| Assault, indecent | 48 | — | 53 | — | 74 | — | 58 | — | 68 | — |
| Assault on females | 51 | — | 51 | 2 | 72 | — | 49 | 1 | 74 | 4 |
| Burglary | 80 | 3 | 96 | 1 | 117 | — | 91 | 3 | 95 | — |
| Carrying unlawful weapons | 15 | — | 17 | — | 34 | — | 48 | — | 107 | 1 |
| Concealing birth and deserting child | 2 | 11 | — | 7 | 2 | 6 | 4 | 7 | 1 | 7 |
| Endangering safety of passengers on railway | 15 | 1 | 10 | — | 12 | — | 28 | — | 19 | — |
| Forgery, etc. | 91 | — | 68 | 2 | 120 | — | 147 | 5 | 172 | 1 |
| Gambling Act, breaches of | 77 | 1 | 105 | 1 | 101 | — | 107 | — | 434 | 2 |
| Horse stealing, etc. | 65 | 2 | 72 | 2 | 66 | 2 | 93 | 2 | 83 | — |
| House and shop breaking | 313 | 3 | 284 | 3 | 345 | 1 | 364 | 2 | 472 | — |
| Larceny | 2,988 | 196 | 2,869 | 235 | 3,064 | 263 | 3,268 | 236 | 3,486 | 288 |
| Malicious injury to horses, etc | 81 | 4 | 72 | 2 | 89 | 6 | 62 | 3 | 63 | 2 |
| Manslaughter | 11 | 1 | 16 | 1 | 14 | — | 19 | 1 | 14 | 1 |
| Murder | 6 | 1 | 11 | — | 8 | 1 | 14 | — | 11 | 1 |
| Prison breach, escape, etc | 48 | 1 | 62 | — | 62 | 1 | 70 | — | 64 | 3 |
| Refusing to support family | 38 | 1 | 37 | 1 | 44 | 1 | 53 | 1 | 59 | 1 |
| Robbery | 51 | 1 | 29 | — | 80 | 1 | 92 | — | 83 | 1 |
| Shooting and wounding | 105 | 4 | 78 | 3 | 105 | 5 | 109 | 2 | 101 | 3 |
| Suicide, attempt at | 10 | 2 | 12 | 8 | 22 | 1 | 21 | 4 | 21 | 7 |

*Canada Year Book, 1906, p. 478*

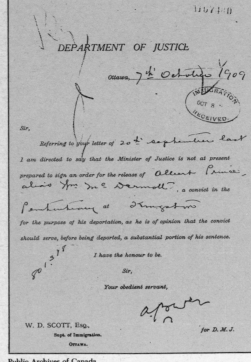 Public Archives of Canada

John Knowles, a small rancher on Willow Creek . . . was charged on the information of his accomplice, Daniel Dixon . . . with stealing one calf . . . Daniel Dixon pleaded guilty, and was sentenced to two years at Stony Mountain, and Knowles, upon conviction, was given ten years at the same place. (1905) L. G. Thomas, *The Prairie West*, p. 252

*Part of the Edmonton police force, 1913*

# POLICE

*Division, Lethbridge, Alberta, 1893.*

## Jail

The cells at police headquarters were filled to their utmost capacity last night, no less than seventy men, besides a number of women, finishing up their Thanksgiving celebrations behind the bars. A number of others were bailed by their friends, and judging from the number of battered and bleeding faces seen in the station duty office, there were others who ought to have been there and some of whom likely will be.

A reporter who visited the cells at 3 o'clock this morning found that less than half of the prisoners were provided with beds. There are seventeen cells for male prisoners, and these were so crowded that many of the men were spending the night lying on the concrete floor, while others paced to and fro behind the bars like wild beasts in a cage. Some prisoners lay in a drunken sleep; others, half-sobered, made night hideous with their attempts to sing. 'We shall meet on that beautiful shore' being the favorite hymn at the time the reporter called. Among the prisoners were a few sober, respectably dressed men, and with no bed, no quiet and the company of drunken cell-mates, they appeared to have little cause for thanksgiving. *Winnipeg Free Press*, Oct. 25th, 1909.

J. S. Woodworth, *My Neighbour*, p. 140

## Juvenile Crime

One of the principals of the public schools states: 'I have noted during the past five years that many children leave school to go to work long before they are physically fit or have any adequate preparation for their life work. Very few children in our district complete the eighth grade in school (i.e., the public school course). They go to work in stores, box factories, breweries and as messenger and office boys. Many girls and boys are kept at home to mind younger children while the parents are out working. It is a sad fact, but it seems necessary that in order to maintain the existence of a family the mother must go out to work rather than care for her children. This is the source of much truancy and juvenile crime.'

J. S. Woodworth, *My Neighbour*, p. 68

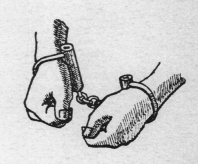

## The Mounties

During the early days of settlement the cause of law and order was well served by what was later to be known as the Royal North West Mounted Police but which in the early days were known as the NWMP or Mounties, the members of this most efficient force often acting in the multiple capacities of prosecutor, counsel for the defence, judge, jury and executioner, which not only tended to the general satisfaction of all concerned but also saved the Department of Justice considerable sums of money that otherwise would have been expended in bringing cases of alleged wrong doing before a duly constituted court. But as settlement increased there seemed to grow up a desire, on the part of some, for a more complicated and formal method of procedure.

H. Robertson, *Salt of the Earth*, p. 116

| SUMMARY CONVICTIONS FOR OFFENCES, 1901 – 1905 | | | | | |
|---|---|---|---|---|---|
| **Offences** | 1901 | 1902 | 1903 | 1904 | 1905 |
| | No. | No. | No. | No. | No. |
| Assault | 3,093 | 2,970 | 3,394 | 3,611 | 3,621 |
| Breach of peace | 708 | 833 | 976 | 977 | 1,021 |
| Cruelty to animals | 282 | 297 | 366 | 476 | 444 |
| Drunkenness | 12,725 | 13,324 | 16,532 | 18,895 | 21,621 |
| Highways, offences relating to | 185 | 437 | 540 | 704 | 1,057 |
| Insanity | 120 | 110 | 143 | 148 | 270 |
| Insulting, Obscene and profane language | 596 | 549 | 644 | 593 | 729 |
| Liquor license acts, offences against | 2,230 | 2,366 | 3,031 | 3,018 | 3,275 |
| Municipal acts and bylaws, breaches of | 4,974 | 4,885 | 5,240 | 4,562 | 6,273 |
| Threats and abusive language | 355 | 424 | 434 | 659 | 398 |

*Canada Year Book*, 1906, p. 479